SHIFT
DIRECTION

Find your way to the job you love

Lorraine Purbrick

CONTENTS

Dedicated to
Sam and Josh,
my lovely boys

Foreword

To be invited to write a foreword to Lorraine Purbrick's book about how to approach the changes both chosen and thrust upon us, feels like a real privilege. Lorraine was a skilled and creative Executive Coach for many years and brought inspiration to her many clients.

The philosophy and practical steps offered in this book will be of real help to people wishing to enter into change in a state of awareness, curiosity and with a sense of wanting to learn deeply about themselves and to grow in the process.

The basis for the book is not theoretical it has come from direct experience of change, both chosen and not chosen, by Lorraine and her contributing colleagues. Lorraine was an inspiration to me as she faced cancer with courage and optimism, while still selflessly supporting others in their own journeys both in their professional and personal lives.

Even in the last days of her life, as her illness exhausted her, she was fulfilling her desire to help others by sharing her wisdom and knowledge of some effective ways to meet life's challenges. I recommend this book to you as a fine resource, whether like Lorraine you are a coach, a facilitator or... a human being on their journey... as of course are we all.

Victoria Cassells, Executive Coach

Preface

By profession, I am an executive coach and facilitator accredited by APECS (Association for Professional Executive Coaching and Supervision). I have now been working in my 'dream job' for over 15 years. I have had the good fortune of working for a large corporate financial institution for over 13 years, a well-known public transport company for seven years, as well as a host of other businesses.

This book is about the lessons I've learned on the journey I took to get to my 'dream job'. In the process I distilled a model for helping other people do the same, the SHIFT model, and my hope is this will help you to find your dream job more easily.

I have been working with this model, first with myself, and then with others as a coach, in evolving formats since the early 1990s. It's been so exciting seeing people transition to work they love. Yet life hasn't worked out as I expected, and that also forms part of the story.

In 2011, when my children were 8 and 5, I was diagnosed with breast cancer. Then in 2014 I developed a brain tumour. For five years, as a family, we've lived with the uncertainty of my recovery, which has affected us all in different ways. It has helped me to focus on my 'legacy' to my husband, children, nieces and nephews, godchildren and friends, but also to my wider working community.

We tend to live assuming we are going to be around until we are 80 or so. Yet this is not always the case. My motto after cancer is to 'live for now'. But why wait until you have a life-threatening illness to really think about your legacy? Thankfully for me, I have been working in my dream job for quite a while. So this book documents part of my legacy to people I have worked with over the years. I want to pass on what I have learnt about finding a fulfilling role so that others, including my sons, can do the same.

What are you doing to reach your dream job? What will you be passing on to the next generation? Don't leave it too late!

Lorraine Purbrick
1966-2017

Acknowledgements

I wrote this book following a diagnosis of a brain tumour in 2014 and I managed to complete the first draft. My thanks go to James Lawrence who then edited my work when I became too ill to continue. Without him this book would not be in print, forming part of my legacy.

Two coaching colleagues, Clare Hester and Jani Rubery have been a huge encouragement. Clare has used the model in this book on herself and then began to use it with clients. They have both added valuable contributions towards the editing process and I am particularly thankful for their overall encouragement and enthusiasm. I am delighted that they are now involved in SHIFT as career coaches.

My thanks finally go to my husband Rob, for his support in producing this book with the help of his friends, David Lund, who designed the front cover, Rory Keegan who was proof-reader, and Chris Powell and the team at Verité CM Ltd who undertook the typesetting.

Introduction

What will your legacy be?

This might seem an odd place to start a book about finding the occupation you love. However, very few of us give much thought to what we will leave behind after we have gone. What will be our legacy? What will we be remembered for? How have we influenced those around us using our gifts and talents? Many people, even when they reach their eighties, have never really thought about their legacy.

My uncle died recently. His legacy was being a true gentleman, committed to his wife in health and sickness until she died, a man of integrity and true to his word, a man who lived out his faith right to the end, and who had a number of long-standing trusted friends who stuck by him no matter what – he was obviously a good friend too.

He was a quantity surveyor before he retired. I have no idea how good he was at his job or how successful he was, other than it took him quite a while to pass all his exams and he worked for a number of years for one firm. What mattered to me was his example of good character, his commitment as a husband to his wife, as an uncle (he had no children of his own) and as an example of how to keep long-standing friends.

So before thinking about our career legacy, it's important first to consider our own character, and how we might be inspiring others who are close to us to live well, and then our commitment to our spouse and children, if we have either of those. After that comes our calling to our career, what we are designed to be, finding the job that most gives us energy and life, something that we cannot stop ourselves doing. And in so doing, we leave behind even more of a legacy for the next generation and those around us.

The reality is sobering. Illness or injury can hit suddenly. What we currently take for granted may not be possible in the future. A friend of ours died quite suddenly from a brain haemorrhage in his early fifties, leaving a wife, son and daughter. Another had a sudden stroke in his forties and his mental abilities were reduced to those of a child. Physically he is unable to work in the City and his wife is left struggling to look after him and their two children under five. Another person I know was diagnosed with cancer at the age of 14. Having survived her treatment, she is now studying to be a cancer research scientist.

Whilst we all have legacies, good and bad, why wait for a life-threatening illness to think about your legacy?

The journey

Before I became a wife and mother, I focused much of my time discerning what I loved doing most and then plotting a route to make it my profession, where work became my hobby so I never had to work again. Once I discerned my dream job it took me longer than I would have liked to get there – eight years in all. I have come to trust, from my own experience and from helping others, that it is the journey that matters, not how quickly we arrive at the destination. The timing is not up to me, just the perseverance to keep going in the right direction. Then eventually I will get there.

Imagine you are gazing at a place you really want to go to, off in the distance. All that stands between you and your dream destination is a fast-flowing river that you have to cross on foot, via stepping stones. It's a place you have thought about often; in fact you've so many ideas of how it might feel and look that it's driving you to distraction not being there.

However to get across the river, you need to take some risks. There are people you could ask for guidance, but nobody can do it for you. You have to take the first step yourself. You tentatively look over your shoulder and take a deep breath. The first stepping stone is certainly large enough for you to place both feet on. It's wide under the water and very stable. But for some reason, even though it's a small step physically, it takes great courage and some cheering from onlookers to leave the bank of the river and firmly place both feet on the stone.

From a distance it's hard to make out the farthest stones. You find yourself wondering whether they will be stable, sufficient to hold your weight and all you need to carry. You press on to the next stone, growing in confidence as you make progress and see how far you've come. At some points there are a number of steps you could take, each taking you in a different direction. Some are so large you can sit down and take a rest for a while. Sometimes the direction to take is only obvious when you are virtually on top of it, so close there is no doubt. Had you tried to see that step at the start you would not have been able to find it, but now you are moving in the right direction you are certain it will get you where you want to be.

As long as the next stone takes you in the right direction – closer to the dream destination – you make step changes until you eventually get to the other side. Each stone needs testing before you put your full weight on it. There are always others to help along the way. Perhaps it's people who have taken this route before, or those further down the river who can see from an alternative, helpful perspective.

In your career, taking each step whilst checking you are going in the right direction is the essence of this process. Sometimes these stepping stones will feel unsafe and wobbly, others may seem to lead you in the wrong direction, other steps may be essential for money reasons until you are free to get back on track, doing what you are designed to do. The whole journey may seem time-consuming and longer than you wished, but maybe there is something to learn from the journey's frustrations to help you reach your dream destination. At such moments it helps to get all the support you can until another stepping stone emerges that feels right, and then you persevere until you are on the other side. If time runs out on you before you reach the other side, at least you are on a purposeful journey making step changes as they emerge, working with more of the skills and passions that you love.

This book is structured to take you on this journey.

Part 1 Telling stories

In Chapter 1 I tell my own story and reflect on the lessons I've learned along the way. Although I practiced as an executive coach and facilitator for over 15 years supporting individuals and teams within a business context, I never once marketed myself as a career coach. Yet people would come to me wanting to explore their future career, and my approach to helping them evolved. It felt like a calling. When I worked this way, I was immensely satisfied seeing clients move forward and achieve more than they ever thought possible. As my supervisor, Victoria Cassells, once told me: 'Eighty per cent of what we do as an executive coach is holding the belief for our clients that they can reach their goal'. This is what she did for me, even though it took me eight years from being a graduate trainee to an executive coach. Yet that wasn't the end of the journey.

I go on to describe the rest of my journey. I became a wife and mother, and I realised my significance was still tied up in my hobby – work. When the children came along I stopped paid employment for a while and later worked flexibly around their school times. It was during this time I realised my core identity was not primarily connected with the work I did, but was to be found in who I was as a person. We know this in our heads, but when work is stripped away for whatever reason, who are we? Are we secure and significant just as we are, without having to justify our existence as a lawyer, manager or teacher? Who we are is always more important than what we do.

This early lesson in security and significance was taken to a new depth when I developed breast cancer in 2011 and then secondary cancer in the brain in 2014. This was also the time I began really to focus on my legacy. After a breast cancer diagnosis you live with the hope of being cured. You hope and pray for the best, trying to beat the five- and ten-year milestones.

I was diagnosed with secondary breast cancer three years later, and told it was incurable. My days were numbered. Whilst every patient is different, I am surprising my oncologist at how long I am lasting following my brain tumour operation, which left me unable to walk, see properly, talk properly or move my head without causing motion sickness.

During my recovery, as I began to regain the ability to see again, reading and typing became a possibility. Whilst my focus was always first and foremost as a wife and mother, in my spare time I began to write this book. It felt like a chance to make sense of my work, a chance to pass on the model I have used to help others find their true gifting and career path, a chance to leave a legacy.

In Chapter 2 I tell some stories of others who I have helped on their journey to a dream job, and reflect on insights we can gain through their experience.

Part 2 The models

In Part 2 of this book I describe the process that I developed for myself, and have then used with others, which helps people find the job they love.

Whilst eating well, exercising well and leading a balanced life are all important to living well, when we find the job we love, we are naturally energised, discover a deep sense of satisfaction and feel good about ourselves. This contributes to our sense of wellbeing and how we cope with stress. I have seen too many people 'burn out' from being in the wrong job or in the wrong working environment. The stress and illness this creates not only has a huge effect on them, but also on those around them.

We spend around eighty per cent of our waking time at work. If we're content at work it is bound to spill over into the rest of our lives. If we're not content, that will spill over as well.

Which of the following statements best describe your attitude about your work right now[1]?

☐ Dream job

☐ Thumbs up

☐ Mustn't grumble

☐ Someone's got to do it

☐ I am stuck

☐ I have drifted into this job

☐ I am lacking in confidence and don't know where to start getting a job

☐ Wage slave

Most people are probably in a job best described by the bottom six labels. This book offers a process to explore what you are designed to do and identifies steps to get there, so that you might tick one of the top two labels for your work role. It focuses on two models, and then explores some of the challenges you might expect to face along the way.

1. Identify your SHIFT profile (Chapter 3)

The SHIFT model has been developed through years of working as a coach with many different clients, and also through insights gained from three well-known books about how to get the job you love. My aim with this model has been to pick the best from each approach and simplify the process for you, making it quicker and easier to discern a vision of your ideal career. If you want to dig deeper, I recommend the following books:

- *What Colour is your Parachute?* Richard N Bolles

- *Purpose Driven Life*, Rick Warren

- *How to Get a Job you Love*, John Lees

The SHIFT model has been born out of personal experience working on my own career path as well as supporting others through change in theirs. It explores your:

S – Skills and talents

H – Heart, what you are most passionate about

I – Interests, knowledge and experience areas

F – Fears and blocks to action

T – Type and traits of your personality

This process is opposite to how most of us look for a new job. Too often we look at a job specification and think how we can best fit into that role and prove we are right for the job. The SHIFT process requires you to start with who you are. What are you naturally gifted at? What can't you stop yourself doing? What are the skills you love using? Many of my clients have found that once they have worked out their top gifts, they change little over time, only maybe a small amount due to life circumstances. This is because this is who they really are and who they are designed to be.

Whilst you can attempt to work through the SHIFT model on your own, I strongly advise that you find a career guide who can work alongside you as your career coach and hold you accountable for your actions. I have helped many people change career using SHIFT and most, if not all, have appreciated the support and encouragement of a listening ear, simply reflecting back their thoughts. The career guide does not need to be a qualified coach (although that would definitely help). However make sure you choose someone who can:

- Listen and reflect
- Remain on your agenda for the whole session
- Meet you for at least four ninety-minute sessions
- Believe in you as a person.

When I was working out my own SHIFT pattern, I spent many hours pouring over books, but if you are a verbal processor who prefers to discover your thoughts as you speak them, then you may find that a Career Guide is a much better option for you. If you are not sure how to find such a guide, visit my website *www.shift-direction.com* for a range of trained SHIFT coaches who, depending on their experience, are executive coaches or career coaches.

I have detailed different options in Chapter 3 to help you work out your SHIFT pattern, depending on how you like to work best – with, or without, a Career Guide.

2. Identifying your ideal working environment (Chapter 4)

Once you have used the SHIFT model to identify what you want to do with your career, you can then discern the ideal environment in which you will thrive. The environment matters, as you can be in the right job – even your ideal job – but working for the wrong boss or with the wrong type of person can have a negative impact on your wellbeing and progress. Seven out of ten people leave their jobs because of a bad boss.

This chapter explores:

- Ideal role – Given your SHIFT pattern, what ideal roles might be a good fit for you
- Boss/colleagues – What type of people enable you to thrive at work?

- Geography – Where in the world do you want to work? How long are you prepared to commute?

- Environment – What is your preferred physical environment, e.g. office/ home, open plan/ closed offices, location of workplace?

- Salary – What is the minimum or ideal salary you need in order to support yourself/ your family?

Then you can start networking looking for your ideal role or your next role that takes you one step closer to building up the skills you need, using your SHIFT pattern as a guide to make sure you are on the right track.

Chapter 5 looks at how to change jobs using the insights gained from working through your SHIFT model and identifying your ideal workplace, contrasting the approach taken by employers with the approach that really works for you.

Part 3 The challenges

Life rarely goes as smoothly as we would like, so in Part 3 I explore a range of challenges that we are likely to experience on our journey. Chapter 6 considers illness, both physical and mental, through my own story and the stories of others. Chapter 7 explores adversity, Chapter 8 considers how we juggle work and family, and Chapter 9 discusses what to do when there is no ideal job available.

SHIFT Direction Workbook

It will help you to make notes and summarise your findings as you work through the SHIFT model. Keep all the information in one place so that you can use it as a checklist as you move from one stepping stone to another.

To aid this process I have produced an A4 workbook that compliments this book. It is available via the website: www.shift-direction.com. It has all the work sheets as well as some useful additional material.

Coaching Buddies and SHIFT Career Coaches

I strongly suggest that you find a coaching buddy or professional career coach to help you process the exercises in this book. Whilst you can work through the exercises on your own, drawing your own conclusions, there are limitations to this approach. Without another's perspective your thinking and options that come to mind, will be limited by what you have encountered up to that point.

A coaching buddy works well if you know someone that will challenge you and help you think creatively about your options.

A SHIFT career coach is my recommendation if you want to work with a professional who knows the material well and will support and challenge you to get the most from SHIFT.

If you do not know someone appropriate or you think you would like a professional career coach to help you, we have a team of experienced SHIFT coaches available to support you. Please go to the website: www.shift-direction.com for information on the coaches, how the coaching process works and fee structure.

Note of caution

The process of transitioning from one role to another can take many steps. It may take several months or even years. Begin by working out your ideal SHIFT pattern and environment you like working in best through these two models. Then every time you apply for another role you can use your summary as a checklist to make sure you are moving in the right direction, using more skills or gaining more experience in your quest of realising your long-term vision and purpose.

The process works, even if it takes time. I am proof that you can get the job you love, be paid for it and never have to 'work' again!

Enjoy the journey.

Part 1

TELLING **STORIES**

Chapter 1
My story

My own experience of discerning my dream job involved a series of stepping stones, initially into my early career, and then on to a clarified sense of what I really wanted to do, which included the support of a mentor and taking further qualifications.

In this chapter I identify some of my own learning points as a way of illustrating what such a journey can look like.

1. Discern your natural talents

Identify natural talents

As a child, the one thing I knew I was good at was sport. From a very young age I was hitting, kicking and throwing balls wherever and whenever I could. It came so naturally to me, just like a duck swimming in water, and because I was good at sport, it gave me a confidence and joy to keep doing more of it. This was not something I learnt, it was a gift that I was born with.

My father encouraged me to try different sports: at the age of seven I started playing squash.

As I got older my love of squash grew. I found it to be a great source of enjoyment, physical and mental exertion, and a therapeutic release of anger and tension, all rolled into one forty-five minute game, I gradually became more proficient, and by the age of thirteen I was beating my father and giving him points as a head start.

I also came to realise that although I had a natural ability at squash, and my father's enthusiasm and encouragement had got me a long way, I now needed to learn the right techniques to excel at the sport. I was selected for the county under-14s squad where coaching corrected my grip and improved my technique. I continued to play for the county and later the England Universities team.

For reflection

When considering what you want to do in your career, a good starting place is to consider your natural talents. These are the 'things that you cannot help yourself from doing', and they are a good clue as to where your success will lie. They are part of who you are: using these skills naturally gives you joy.

Develop talents

However, talent alone is not going to make you successful. In his book Growing Leaders, James Lawrence states that it is *natural talent combined with knowledge and skills* that leads to success[i]. I may have been naturally talented at squash but to be successful I had to acquire the necessary knowledge (technique) and hone my skills through drills and exercises.

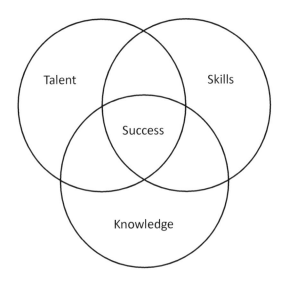

2. Build on your talents and diversify

While I loved squash, a back injury in my late teens meant that I was never going to have a career in sport. I did, however, pursue coaching qualifications and became the Bath University women's squash coach during my student years. For me, this was a natural progression – from playing the sport to helping others play – and it was also a whole lot more interesting and rewarding than waitressing as a student job.

I discovered that coaching was something else that came naturally to me. I loved it with a passion and grew a women's team from nothing (my only option had been to play for the university men's team), recruiting and encouraging players to compete in the county leagues for the first time. Little did I know it at the time, but this was my first taste of coaching, a profession which I would later pursue in the business world.

3. Seek out companies that invest in people

Despite discovering that coaching was something that felt very natural to me, I realised that I was never going to make a career out of squash coaching. I was studying food microbiology at the time but could not see myself working in laboratories either. After several work placements, I managed to get myself onto a graduate training scheme with Unilever, as a technical marketing manager.

'When in doubt pick a good company that will invest lots of money in training you and it will serve you well' – this was sound advice from a friend, Jane, who was a very successful business woman.

At Unilever, I was trained in management and leadership skills while managing and launching global hand-wash products, amongst other things. I learned a range of skills, such as forecasting, budgeting, promoting, briefing agencies, and making presentations. Although I could never get very excited about the actual product – soap – the experience and training was invaluable, and years later, Unilever's presence on my coaching profile still speaks volumes.

Yet I was still acutely aware that what I loved doing was coaching. This was so far removed from my marketing job; I started to look for ways to take a step in that direction within Unilever.

4. Find yourself a mentor who believes in you

After two years at Unilever, I received training from an executive coach and management consultant, Victoria Cassells. Victoria's job appeared to epitomise what I wanted to do. She helped my graduate cohort to understand our personality profiles and grow in communication skills. She had a unique presence that captivated me and a compelling congruence and style that I wanted to emulate.

I was clearer than ever before that this was what I wanted to do for a job. I decided to pluck up the courage to find out how I might go about this. After one of Victoria's training sessions, I asked for her contact details and if we could meet up. Kindly she agreed, and we met for one of the most engaging and exciting conversations of my professional career.

During our meeting I asked her many questions about her job including:

- What did she like about her job?
- What were the pitfalls?
- What was it like to work in her coaching company?
- What career moves would I need to make to gain sufficient credibility to do her job?

After our meeting, I was buzzing! I remember driving away from the hotel on a real high. I had finally found a vision of what I wanted to do and had worked out some steps to get there, despite the reality that I was still a marketing manager with no experience in business coaching and facilitation.

After my meeting with Victoria, I kept in touch with her three or four times a year and over time she became my mentor, supervisor and close friend. She believed in me even when my confidence wavered. It was her single belief in me that gave me the courage to carry on towards my goal of becoming an executive coach. It doesn't take everyone as long as me to transition. Remember, I wasn't long out of university when I worked out where I wanted to go with my career.

For reflection

Purely holding a belief in somebody can make all the difference in supporting them to reach their ideal role. When you find a mentor who can do this for you, you have struck gold. Better still, when you hold this belief for someone else, it is wonderful to see the fruit.

My definition of a mentor is someone who has more experience than you in the role or industry in which you want to work. They have the ability to come along side you, encourage, listen, and sometimes just be with you[iii].

A mentor differs from a coach, who will have more experience in coaching skills and perhaps psychological theory, and will similarly come alongside you but may not have experience in the specific role or industry you are seeking to enter.

In my case, Victoria had both mentoring and coaching capabilities, so I am fortunate that she has been by my side over the last twenty-two years.

5. Develop your natural skills outside your core role

So there I was, stuck in my Unilever marketing role, wanting to do coaching and facilitation, and yet my main role was launching global soap products into the UK market. All my efforts to transfer to a Human Resources (HR) function came to a dead end, so the only option remaining was to develop my skills within the role I had.

I had recently transferred to the Food and Beverage Hygiene Department, where the sales team had just lost a big contract for a very large and well-known drinks company. The feedback was that they had not 'listened' to the brief and consequently had lost an important client. As a result it was deemed that there was a need for sales training on influence and persuasion techniques.

Even though I was the marketing manager for this division, I persuaded the Sales Director that I could co-design and deliver a three-day training course with a coach from Victoria's company. This on-the-job training was a fantastic opportunity for me to learn from an expert and receive feedback about my coaching and facilitation skills. At the end of the three days I was exhausted but on a high. I knew that this was the best piece of work I had done so far, and it confirmed that this was the role that I wanted to do in the long term.

Furthermore, the transformation in the sales team was equally exciting. As they became more self-aware about their own communication skills, new ideas about how to approach new contracts began to surface, which, when they put them into practice, led them to win more contracts.

For reflection

Where possible, work at developing and expanding your skills in your current role. Everything you can do in your current role helps you develop experience that you can add to your CV or profile, particularly if you are trying to transfer to a different role or a different industry.

6. Develop your skills outside work

Another way to gain experience in tasks more suited to your personality and preferences is to seek opportunities outside of work. I loved coaching and yet had little opportunity to do it in my marketing role, so I began offering free coaching for friends and colleagues who were also in a state of flux with their careers.

During my search for 'what next' after my marketing role (there is only so much soap you can handle) I worked through some of the exercises in the book What Colour is Your Parachute?[iv] With a little help from a career coach, I discerned the Top 10 skills that I actually loved using and discovered a range of other skills that I liked, but did not give me much energy or joy when I used them. This was the start of a process that became known as the SHIFT model (see Chapter 3), which I used first on myself and then practised on others.

Practising on friends and colleagues, outside of work, helped me to gain confidence and hone my process. Coaching others also gave me a real sense of achievement. It was definitely what I wanted to do next, but I was still going to struggle to convince a new employer that I was any good at coaching and facilitation when my CV was mostly about marketing soap.

7. Changing your role is a step-by-step process

When considering how to change from one role and industry to another, I recommend Daniel Porot's diagram from *What Colour is My Parachute?*[v].

Changing roles and industries

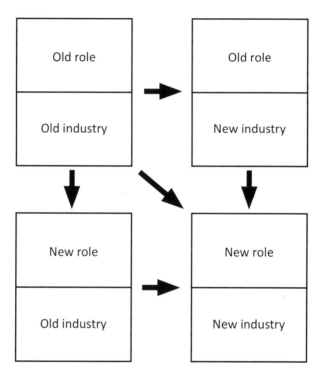

I was starting in the top left box, my 'old' job was marketing and my 'old' field was the food and drink industry.

To move directly to a 'new role' of coaching in a 'new industry' was a difficult path from where I was (following the diagonal arrow from top left to bottom right). An easier path was to move to a company perhaps in the same industry but with a different role or to a different industry but with same role.

I had already tried to move to HR within Unilever and this door was firmly closed. I then had the opportunity to join a food and grocery institute (remaining in my old industry) that delivered research and training to global food manufacturers.

The main reason I was recruited was not only my marketing background, but also because I was a food microbiologist by training. They needed a scientific researcher to provide impartial information and training on genetically modified foods to consumers. It reminded me that nothing is ever wasted – even my food microbiology degree came in handy at this point.

The main reason I joined was because my research job was a 'way in' to the company, and once in I hoped to influence them to grow my role into more training and facilitation. After a year or so I did just that, and by the time I left I was heading up the training and development department delivering nine different training courses in the UK and Europe.

I also became the Institute's coach for the internal training team, once again recruiting Victoria's company to co-design and deliver communication skills training, Once again I was building my capability alongside my main role.

For reflection

When you have worked through the SHIFT model and developed a clear picture of your ideal role (Chapter 3), begin to think about the steps necessary for you to gain credibility and experience in reaching your end goal.

One of the gaps in my experience, having only had marketing roles until my research role, was client-facing time. Client-handling experience was another reason I took up my research post. Through the bespoke training and facilitation for big global suppliers, I gained some useful skills in relationship management, proposal writing, negotiating, persuading, sales and so on. These were all necessary for my long-term role as an executive coach.

8. Going for gold: adopting your new role in a new industry

Finding myself bored with the training courses I was delivering was a sure sign it was time to move on. This was my chance to take the next step in the career path to coaching/facilitation in an industry away from food and grocery. I fell into the banking industry, rather than deliberately choosing it.

As I had little corporate experience outside the food and drink industry, I joined an established coaching company as an associate. At the time, in 2000, coaching was very embryonic in companies. However, I had two directors who believed in me and trusted me to develop a coaching process for a large financial institution. As it turned out, I would work for this company in different capacities for the following thirteen years.

For reflection

If you are branching out as a freelancer or employee in your chosen field and industry, consider whose reputation you can work under whilst you gain more experience. This is a helpful way to achieve big client names to increase your credibility for your next role.

In my case, I knew of the coaching company because one of the directors was the father of our vicar. This led to my associate position with them, and from there I was able to grow my confidence in my skills and knowledge so that my talent could be put to use. After a while, I began to realise what I brought to the role, what I was worth and with whom I wanted to work.

9. Grow your knowledge

One of the pieces of advice Victoria gave me to support my coaching was to explore Gestalt psychotherapy. To begin a Masters in Gestalt psychotherapy meant investing a lot of time and money, which I could only do if I went freelance and worked as an Associate rather than in a full-time role. I coached four days a week, and spent the other working day studying. Gestalt became the bedrock for my coaching work and still is today[vi].

I was developing and honing my skills through my work as a coach and facilitator, while my Masters course was developing the knowledge to underpin those skills. Coupled with my natural love (talent) of coaching, initially sparked by squash coaching all those years ago, I was beginning to live out the skills, knowledge and talent dynamic.

I began to fly, loving the work I was doing and being successful by just being me. In fact, it wasn't work at all, it was fun, a hobby that I was paid to do. I gained more energy from working than I did from anything else and I have never had to 'work' again.

For reflection

For some people it might be possible to grow an area of knowledge alongside your job. Other people take the plunge, give up work for a year and undertake an MBA or similar. Whatever it takes, does it move you one step closer to your chosen career in the industry in which you want to work?

10. Keep networking

I have found networking is one of the keys to getting new roles within the same industry or in other industries. When I was a student looking for a work placement, I networked with a friend's sister who had links with Unilever. I found a placement with Birds Eye Walls (a Unilever company), which later led to my recruitment onto the marketing graduate trainee programme with Unilever.

Whilst my research job came from answering an advert, it was a friend who saw the ad for me. Get your family and friends to keep their eyes open on your behalf. My move to become an associate executive coach and trainer came through networking with the company directors, who I knew through a church link.

Most, if not all, of the sales that I generate as a freelance executive coach come as a result of networking and developing a genuine interest in other people. Over 15 years, I have not needed to invest in a website or even a business card because building trust in relationships is what matters most.

On reflection

Every story is unique, and inevitably you will connect with parts of mine and not with others, but I wanted to share it with you in some detail, to illustrate one journey from start to finish through the process of finding the job you love. So now let's take a look at some other people's stories and how they discovered their dream job using the SHIFT model. For each of these case studies, I was just one link in the chain of change. There are many steps to a career change, and it requires you to develop a vision and persevere in taking steps towards it, however long it takes. The journey starts here.

Chapter 2
Their story

In this chapter I have selected three of my clients who have used the SHIFT model successfully over the last decade or two. I have listed some of the learning points from each case study for you to consider for your own journey. Often the process of articulating their journey has helped them affirm what they already knew about themselves as well as gain greater clarity about what they 'want' for the future.

A core concept of Gestalt therapy is that 'change happens when we become more of who we are', or, in other words, more of who we are designed to be. These people have used the SHIFT model to help them get closer to that ideal. Once they were clear on the right direction to head in, they were able to map the steps to get there, or at least look for the first stepping stone heading in that direction. As Steven Covey says in The Seven Habits of Highly Effective People: 'If the ladder is not leaning against the right wall, every step we take just gets us to the wrong place faster.'

Yet the journey is rarely easy. Some people get stuck part way through this process, as they cannot quite believe they could ever make a career out of their ideal role. For some people there will be big emotional roadblocks, fears and assumptions, which, unless they are addressed, will always trip them up. One client I had saw himself as a victim most of the time, throughout different stages of his life. As much as we explored his SHIFT model and despite a clear vision of what would excite him in his work, he could not move from 'victim mentality' to 'overcomer' mentality. He really needed to address this emotional (and perhaps spiritual) block before change was going to happen.

Read the stories below of people who have trusted the process and gone with the flow in pursuit of their ideal role. It may take time to reach your ideal job. Remember, the path there has no specific time line. Enjoy the journey, 'live for now' and know that nothing is wasted – it's all helpful learning, even the blind alleys. Just trust the process.

Story 1: Sarah, from administrator to MD of award-winning charity

Not long after graduating from university, I worked as the head of a UK-wide communications project for a non-profit organisation. I was responsible for running thirteen different projects, each involving a conference and an advertising campaign. I loved it. I was using my marketing qualification and learning skills across a wide variety of activities.

Whilst I loved the job, the hours were gruelling. Over time, the personal cost of this amazing job began to stack up. My boss presented an additional set of problems. While she behaved wonderfully outside of work, she had a completely different persona in the office. As I discovered later, her personality profile was the opposite from mine. This meant that, whilst we had complementary methods of working, she was always going to be challenging for me to work with unless we could learn to appreciate our differences. Her management style left me feeling useless – imprecise and with poor attention to detail. These qualities are strengths of her personality profile and – as I later discovered – opposite to mine, which are social, dynamic, and persuasive.

However, this bad experience showed me how differently I wanted to lead, manage a team and generate an alternative kind of organisational culture. It was at this point that I met Lorraine, whilst working on a project with her husband Rob. Over a series of sessions we explored my ideal role using the SHIFT model. I discovered the gifts that I loved using the most were leading, teaching, coaching, facilitating, speaking and using my intuition. I felt most alive when I was using these gifts, but employed few of them in my current role.

Working through SHIFT revealed that my heart and passion are for leadership and the impact it has on a person's life, either positively or negatively. I also realised I am a generalist who likes to juggle a lot of things but not necessarily specialise. I am very happy for others to be the experts from whose knowledge I can draw.

When exploring my external environment I gained important insights into my preferences. For example, I enjoy starting with a small team and growing it. Money is not that important to me as long as it covers my essential needs. I need to be able to respect my boss who I expect to have certain qualities in order for me to flourish under him or her. It helped to consider a previous senior boss who was a positive influence, rather than just focusing on my current boss.

By this stage in my career I had lost a lot of confidence and did not think I had much to contribute, but now I knew that the things I loved doing were not going to be realised if I stayed in my current role. How was I going to move forward?

I decided that what I was still good at was managing relationships and that I had account management skills that were very transferable. I needed to find an organisation that could use my current skills and provide an environment where I could develop my gifts and passion.

I found a new job working for an inspirational executive coach and motivational speaker. I learned a lot about leadership and the enormous responsibility it entails. If you can communicate creatively enough and involve enough people you can change hearts and minds. After only a year in that role I realised that, while coaching and training were still high on my agenda, I needed more structure and training if I was to progress. I joined another executive coaching and training company, which appeared to offer a similar working ethos and commitment to the integrity of the company.

I started as an account manager, and went through their leadership and management training courses. During one of the courses I ended up coaching one of the directors in an exercise in managing emotions. The director ended up in tears as I was listening to him – this was a high-octane moment as I realised I could do this coaching thing well, and loved it.

I eventually moved sideways within the company and was contracted to undertake an innovation project as an executive coach for one of their big corporate clients. This was a fast-track year for me. I came to understand my personality insights for the first time, which suddenly made sense of my issues with previous bosses, as well as my gifting in leadership coaching and facilitation. This was very freeing and made a difference to my relationships outside work too. Unfortunately, the company began to implode due to the economic climate, and once again I was looking for somewhere new to pursue my vision for my career.

In a short space of time I had two options on the table. One was to go back to my old non-profit organisation, but this time as the head of the international campaign. The other option was scarier. A good friend, Tim, had recently set up a debt advice project and a night shelter for homeless people and was interested in developing a training project for disengaged young people to get them into work. He suggested that I run the project, and I agreed, even though on paper it looked like the more risky option in every way – financially and from a career perspective. Yet it was the job in which I believed I could make the most difference, where I could grow a team from scratch and fulfil my passion of leading and managing others in a positive culture. The other huge positive point was that I knew Tim to be a visionary leader, who could see a possibility and make it happen, having the unusual combination of a strategic mind with an interest in the details. He is very encouraging and not afraid of challenging in a caring way – my perfect boss at last.

I now lead a team of fifty people. I am the Managing Director and Tim is the CEO. He drives the 'big picture' vision and leaves me to manage the team to accomplish it. We work well as a team, complementing and appreciating each other's leadership style. This job also fulfils my heart's passion – if you can communicate creatively enough and involve enough people you can change hearts and minds.

The aim of the project is to support young people (16-24) to lift themselves out of poverty and train them in skills to be successful in finding employment. During this training we help them to identify what we call the 'power mentality' (as opposed to 'victim mentality'). I just love it at the end of the programme when a young person – who would not previously give me eye contact – gives a presentation and says, 'I am not a victim, I do have choices and I have a future.' That really makes my heart sing: it is about personal leadership.

The charity has gone from strength to strength since it was established in 2003 and has won several different awards for the work we do. The best 'award' for me personally was receiving the results of the 'Great Place to Work' leadership survey, which stated that 97% of people loved working in my team.

When I look back to the work I did with Lorraine in 2000, my heart's passion and top skills are still the same: leading and managing others, developing a small team in a safe and empowering culture, to help change hearts and minds. Whilst that is my top priority, I am using my coaching and facilitating skills to manage the team, and now also visiting other charities to support them in their own journeys to successful transformation.

Lessons from Sarah's story

Here are some reflections from Sarah's story to consider for your own career journey:

- A 'bad boss' can ruin even the best of jobs. The impact can affect your health and confidence. Think about moving to a different position inside the same company or to an external position.

- Understand your own personality profile and that of your boss (Insights profile, the *16personalities.com* website, or Myers Briggs Type Indicator are good tools). How can you appreciate and celebrate differences and become the perfect team?

- Spend time identifying your Top 10 skills and your heart's passion – once defined they may modify over time, with different life events, but essentially they stick with you for years to come.

- Identify your transferable skills and use them to manoeuvre yourself into another company where you can grow your gifting and the talents that you love using.

- When you have different career options before you, do not always go for the logical safe option. Explore the risks and ask the question 'Which one do you have more heart for?'

- Pass on your knowledge and experience to others so that they can learn from your own journey – make it part of your legacy and start thinking about this now as it will frame your choices – life can be shorter than you think.

If Sarah was to write a book as her legacy to the next generation she told me it would be about the power that exists in the way we define ourselves and who we believe ourselves to be. If we define ourselves as victims we will always be victims. If we define ourselves as 'over-comers' we will have the opportunity to live life to the full. We will, of course, still suffer in life, but we will retain the possibility of enduring suffering while retaining our joy, hope and freedom.

Considering your legacy as you work out your SHIFT model is an important aspect of the journey and can help you focus your efforts.

Story 2: Martin, from international investment company to small entrepreneurial investment firm

I was working in a financial services firm looking after a team in Europe and Asia managing hedge funds and raising capital for institutional investors in high-risk projects. I was made a partner of the firm, which gave me more autonomy. Soon after this, our company became a subsidiary of a larger US company. The nerve centre then revolved around New York and most decisions were made there away from the original partners in the UK.

When the market crash happened in 2008, we had just hired new people into the team who were highly ambitious and intelligent, although now we had a high cost base and a lower income base. It was a real struggle to keep the profit and loss accounts balanced for that year. With the crash came some senior executive redundancies, which meant more work in my in-tray. Asia was growing and I was spending eight days a month away from home and then travelling to Europe to grow the business there. The new recruits were inexperienced so I was covering some of their work too.

With decision-making taken away from me, more work than I could juggle and a real sense of helplessness, I had more responsibility than ever before, had less control than ever before and made more money than ever before. I began to experience burnout. I was the unhappiest I have ever been.

In my experience burnout meant I was no longer able to make decisions even on the smallest scale, to such an extent that even the easiest of DIY jobs was too much as I was likely to fail (and I am normally quite good at DIY). I experienced high levels of anxiety and depression and the world became colourless. I needed time out so I left the organisation. I was fortunate enough to have sufficient savings to do this.

When I first met Lorraine to explore how to SHIFT my career, it was apparent that I needed to recover more before taking on the process, so we delayed it for a while. When we did start, I found the structure, exercises and feedback from friends and colleagues very encouraging and uplifting. My ideal role that emerged from the SHIFT model acted as a checklist when being headhunted for different jobs. Whilst this was flattering, it was apparent from the work I had done with Lorraine that these jobs did not reflect the role I now had a vision for, and it would have been likely that I would have ended up back in a similar role elsewhere had I not been vigilant about sticking with the insights gained from the SHIFT model.

The model confirmed that the investment role I was in was the right role for my skills, although the environment needed to be much more entrepreneurial. I also needed to make sure I had a work-life balance that was sustainable for my responsibilities outside of work, which included my health and family amongst other things.

After about a year I joined a smaller investment business as a partner, where the managing partner was more entrepreneurial. We have a good working relationship. The company is much smaller and I have greater control over decision-making. One of the drivers for working in this kind of industry for me is the ability to earn sufficient money not only for my family, but to give it away to causes I feel connected and passionate about. This makes it so much more worthwhile and is part of my legacy.

I am now in an 8/10 job whereas before my last job was a 3/10 at best.

Lessons from Martin's story

Here are some reflections from Martin's story to apply to your own career journey:

- If you are experiencing burnout, wait a while to recover before undertaking this process.
- Notice the symptoms of burnout or mental illness and take time to recover (see Chapter 6).
- Working through the SHIFT model may simply affirm your skill set and role that you are in; you do not always need to radically change your career.
- The environment you work in can hugely change your state of wellbeing.
- Consider how your job contributes towards your legacy.

Story 3: Becky, from mum at home to communications editor and facilitator of global conferences

I first got to know Lorraine in 2006, hanging out together at mother and toddler groups with our children. I was in my early thirties, had one son and was expecting my second child. For a variety of reasons (not least motherhood) my career was at a standstill. I had managed to keep working part-time in corporate event management after my first child was born, but I had no sense of direction and felt frustrated as a mostly stay-at-home mother. I had little hope for my future and no idea what I would or could do career-wise when my children were older.

When my second child was a few months old, Lorraine told me about a leadership course that she was preparing to facilitate. It sounded interesting, and I found myself wishing I could attend. But why? I wasn't a leader. I did co-run a women's group at church, but that wasn't really leadership, was it? I was surprised when Lorraine invited me to attend the course, and went along with a mix of interest and trepidation. I felt like such a fraud. When would the other participants find out that I wasn't a leader? Yet I loved the sessions and as the course went on I found myself identifying with the characteristics and strengths of a leader, and growing in confidence.

Part of the course involved mentoring, which turned out to be a challenging yet rewarding opportunity to get to know myself better and work through questions with my mentor. By the end of the course, I longed for further clarity on where I should be heading career-wise, and Lorraine offered to work with me on this.

Using SHIFT, I learned more about myself and the kind of role and environment to which I was suited. The questions and discussions weren't always easy, but they helped me to grow in self-awareness. The work environment diagram helped me to clarify what is important to me, and I still refer to it, ten years on, when thinking about the type of people I want to work with and the kind of environment in which I want to work.

The SHIFT pattern is very revealing. It asks great questions about all parts of your life, to identify the activities and experience that energise you. Previous career-guidance had only considered my academic strengths and professional work experience but ended with less-than-inspiring suggestions about potential careers. However, considering the activities I enjoyed outside of a work environment showed me that I work best when I have the opportunity to be creative, think independently and work with people. I'm a starter-initiator and love to work towards a deadline or project goal, rather than maintaining procedures day in, day out.

Another big insight was that whilst I can do detailed administrative work, it actually drains me, whereas big-picture thinking energises me. I remember feeling excited as Lorraine and I drew up the list of my Top 10 skills. It felt like 'This is who I am and what I can do!' Bringing all these insights together in a summary document gave me an amazing amount of clarity and confidence in what I had to offer.

A little while later, my husband and I moved overseas with our young family, to work in development with a non-profit organisation. Armed with a new self-awareness and confidence, my career took off, albeit still fitting around the needs of my family. The difference was that the part-time work I did now energised me and challenged me to grow in ways I enjoyed. I quickly moved into a leadership role within a small team and found myself in situations that stretched me and took me out of my comfort zone. But now knowing I had what it took, I was able to embrace the opportunities offered to me. My mantra became 'Face the fear and do it anyway.'

The result was that over the last decade I've worked in a fascinating variety of roles in corporate communication, strategic planning, facilitation, and – to my surprise – governance, gathering invaluable skills and experience along the way. In the last two years I've been identified as an emerging leader and given global-level opportunities to develop my skills.

Looking back at my notes from working with Lorraine ten years ago, I'm amazed at how well they describe what I do today. I guess I found my ideal role and SHIFTED to what I am most suited to. I'm now taking a career break as my family transitions back to life in the UK, and studying for an MA in Global Leadership. I'll be looking for a new job next year but I already know I'll be using the SHIFT tools to evaluate the options and decide which is the right path to follow next.

Lessons from Becky's story

Here are some reflections from Becky's story to apply to your own career journey:

- When you are the main child-carer, you can experience hopelessness, a lack of confidence and frustration in relation to your career.

- It takes one person to see your gifts and believe in you, particularly if you do not have the belief in yourself. They hold the belief for you until a time when you can hold it for yourself.

- Find yourself a mentor: someone who will come alongside you and support you as you explore new skills/directions.

- SHIFT raises your awareness to your needs. Often the SHIFT diagram lasts for a long time and uncovers the core of you that does not change much over time. It is who you are.

- SHIFT can bring clarity and give you confidence in what you can offer.

- Face the fear and do it anyway.

On reflection

Here are three different people, from quite varied work backgrounds, each of them stuck in some way or other and seeking a way to SHIFT their careers to something more suited to their giftings, or finding a better environment in which to thrive.

Irrespective of their backgrounds, SHIFT has helped them articulate what they really want to do, what they are perhaps designed to do, and then through our work together, they have managed to believe that change is possible. About 80% of the career work I do with people is purely holding the belief that they can change to become more of who they already are, helping them to remove the blocks in their path.

Changing career is a process that can take time. Some people drift from one job to another with very little planning. I guess that process can work as long as you drift to the next job that excites you most, using more of the skills you love. Although for most, there comes a time of reflection; a time to think, 'Where am I heading? What do I really want to do? What will be my legacy?'

Now it's your turn. Explore Part 2 having learned some of the lessons from these case studies. Whilst you can work through Part 2 on your own, where possible try and recruit a career guide, someone who can work with you through the exercises, hold you to account and share the journey. It is far easier to articulate these exercises to someone else rather than working through them on your own – and it's more fun.

Part 2

THE **MODELS**

Chapter 3
SHIFT

SHIFTing role may well take time, and it may take several career steps to reach your ideal role, but if you do not start with the end in mind you are more likely to drift and never achieve it. Having said that, some people have a preference not to plan and simply make step changes to where their energy next takes them. Either approach is of course fine as long as you arrive at your ideal role, where you are using your giftings to the full, before its too late. Having had cancer at 44, let me encourage you not to assume that you have all the time in the world.

This chapter looks at your SHIFT model and the next chapter looks at your ideal working environment. Imagine a mustard seed. If it is planted in fertile soil and watered, it will naturally flourish. Likewise, the same seed will naturally die if it falls on stony ground or infertile soil. It's obvious really, it's helpful to know what seed we are and then get clearer on the type of soil we need to flourish. Each chapter has a framework you can complete to summarise your findings from the exercises. Once you have completed the exercises in these chapters and summarised them onto your two charts, this will form your checklist to reference when you are looking for your new role. Make sure that each step of your career uses more of your Top 10 skills than the last and equips you further for your ideal role – until you get there.

SHIFT model

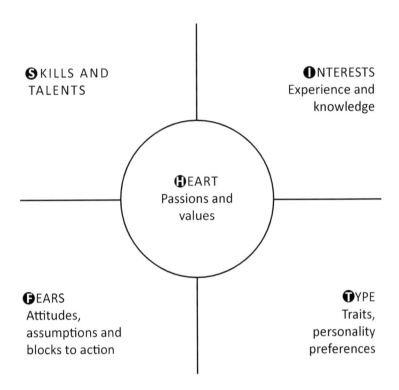

Exploring your SHIFT model – everything about who you are

Developing your SHIFT model is all about WHO you are, what you are naturally good at and what you have a heart for, and also those fears and blocks that often get in the way of you flourishing in pursuit of your ideal role.

S – Skills and talents

H – Heart, what you are most passionate about

I – Interests, knowledge and experience areas

F – Fears and blocks to action

T – Type and traits of your personality

S – defining your Skills and talents

I – discerning your Interests, knowledge and experiences

This section of the SHIFT model on the left, is the most labour-intensive part of the diagram to complete. I have given you two approaches to follow depending on whether or not you have managed to recruit a career guide.

Option 1: Working out your Top 10 skills and talents by yourself

1. Complete the House of Life^{vii}

Complete the House of Life diagram below, taking time to reflect on different stages and roles in your life. Focus on accomplishments and achievements that you have absolutely loved and which gave you a sense of satisfaction – those that have the 'YES' factor for you. Jot down bullet points.

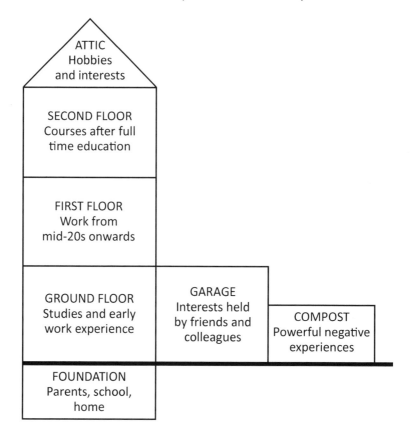

Foundations

- What skills did you learn from your parents?

- What were your favourite subjects at school? What activities and projects did you love to do outside of school?

- What did you find yourself doing in your spare time, which you couldn't stop yourself doing?

Ground floor, first floor, second floor

Reflect upon your career path to date and jot down:

- The training courses that you enjoyed most – what were they and what did you learn?

- Which jobs have you enjoyed the most? What skills did you use in them?

- If your job involves training others, what subjects do you most enjoy?

Attic

Think about your leisure pursuits, areas of personal interest and things you have taught yourself, but which you have stored up and perhaps forgotten about:

- What subjects do you find yourself reading, talking or thinking about with a passion?

- If finances allowed, what area of full-time study would you undertake?

- If money was no object and you did not have to work, what would you actually do to fill the time?

Garage

The garage is on the side because it is about interests you share and admire in others. What do you find attractive in others and want to learn more about? Make a note of these.

Compost

These are experiences which you would usually regard as 'bad' ones but which have been significant in your development, for example burnout, bereavement, illness, dyslexia and so on. It may be that you have learnt much about yourself through these difficulties, grown and been able to give back to others in similar situations. Make a note of these.

2. Capturing the skills and experience from the House of Life

Using small cards or sticky notes look through your House of Life and list all the skills, experience and knowledge you have used (one word per note) at each stage.

3. Compiling your Top 10 skills

1. Now draw three situations on a blank piece of paper (stick people are fine), inside or outside of work where you achieved a 'yes' factor, which was highly satisfying. Try not to think too hard, capture the first three that come to mind.

2. Using more sticky notes, list the skills, knowledge and experience you used in each of the scenarios above. What are the links or themes between these situations? What values emerge?

3. Combine the sticky notes from all these exercises.

4. Now look down the skills list below. Tick off all the skills you love using and list these individually on sticky notes, adding these to your earlier pile.

Skills checklist[viii]

achieving	acting	adapting	addressing
administering	advising	analysing	anticipating
arbitrating	arranging	ascertaining	assembling
assessing	attaining	auditing	budgeting

49

building	calculating	charting	checking
classifying	coaching	collecting	communicating
compiling	completing	composing	computing
conceptualising	conducting	conserving	consolidating
constructing	controlling	coordinating	coping
counselling	creating	deciding	defining
creating	delivering	designing	detailing
detecting	determining	developing	devising
diagnosing	digging	directing	discovering
dispensing	displaying	disproving	dissecting
distributing	diverting	dramatising	drawing
driving	editing	eliminating	empathising
enforcing	establishing	estimating	evaluating
examining	expanding	experimenting	explaining
expressing	extracting	filing	financing
fixing	following	formulating	founding
gathering	generating	getting	giving
guiding	handling	having responsibility	heading
helping	hypothesizing	identifying	illustrating
imagining	implementing	Improving	improvising
increasing	influencing	informing	Initiating
innovating	inspecting	inspiring	installing
instituting	instructing	integrating	interpreting
interviewing	intuiting	inventing	inventory keeping
investigating	judging	keeping	leading

learning	lecturing	lifting	listening
logging	maintaining	making	managing
manipulating	mediating	meeting	memorising
mentoring	modelling	monitoring	motivating
navigating	negotiating	observing	obtaining
offering	operating	ordering	organising
originating	overseeing	painting	perceiving
performing	persuading	photographing	piloting
planning	playing	predicting	preparing
prescribing	presenting	printing	problem solving
processing	producing	programming	projecting
promoting	proofreading	protecting	providing
publicising	purchasing	questioning	raising
reading	realising	reasoning	receiving
recommending	reconciling	recording	recruiting
reducing	referring	rehabilitating	relating
remembering	repairing	reporting	representing
researching	resolving	responding	restoring
retrieving	reviewing	risking	scheduling
selecting	selling	sensing	separating
serving	setting	setting-up	shaping
sharing	showing	singing	sketching
solving	sorting	speaking	studying
summarising	supervising	supplying	symbolising
synergising	synthesising	systematising	taking instructions

talking	teaching	team-building	telling
tending	testing and proving	training	transcribing
translating	travelling	treating	trouble-shooting
tutoring	typing	umpiring	understanding
understudying	unifying	uniting	upgrading
using	utilising	verbalising	weighing
winning	writing		

5. Sort all your sticky notes into the following categories:

☐ Skills I love

☐ Skills I can do (but don't love)

☐ Subject/knowledge areas

☐ Experiences

☐ Dump – skills, experience or knowledge that I no longer want to use

You may have duplicate sticky notes with similar meanings. Combine and distil them into one or two meaningful skills.

From the 'Skills I love' pile, pick out the Top 10 that you absolutely love (would a bit of you die if you were not using them?). I use two ways of prioritising these into a 1-10 order effectively depending on a person's preference.

Method 1 – Using your 'gut' instinct to get your Top 10 skills

With your Top 10 skills on sticky notes and using your gut instinct, decide which of these skills are your number 1 and your number 10. Keep going through the list and order the sticky notes by comparing them to each other so that you have 1-10 skills in priority order. Now add this Top 10 list to the 'Skills and Talent' section of your checklist.

Method 2 – Using a systematic methodology to get to your Top 10 skills

From your pile of 'skills I love' choose ten that are the ones you love the most and then write them down on a piece of paper in any order.

1. Compare each skill against the others to achieve your Top 10 in priority order. For example, from the list below, compare influencing with presenting: which do you prefer? Give it a mark. Compare influencing with analysing. Give it a mark. Once you have compared influencing with all of them, start again with presenting and work down the list again until each skill has been compared with the others, giving you a tally to help you reorder your skills according to priority. For example:

   a. Influencing

   b. Presenting

   c. Analysing

   d. Fixing

2. Now add this Top 10 list to the 'Skills and Talent' section of your checklist.

These exercises will bring to light some valuable knowledge and experiences that you have loved, as well as skills you can do but do not love. It is helpful to keep a record of these sticky notes, for future reference.

When selecting your next role, use your Top 10 skills list as a checklist – how many of these are you using now and how many would you use in the next role? Try to ensure that you are using at least your Top 5 in your next role

I identified my Top 10 skills in 1993 and they are still the same today. The order may have changed a little over time, although the Top 5 haven't. They are the core of who I am and how I am 'wired'.

Option 2: Working out your Top 10 skills with a career guide

If you find it easier to work with a career guide or if you are acting as one for someone else, here are some ideas for a slightly different process. I will refer to the person exploring their career as the career pathfinder.

The career guide needs to be prepared to work with their career pathfinder for a minimum of four sessions, each about ninety minutes long. Helping a career pathfinder to discern their skills usually takes up the first session and takes the longest of all the sections of the SHIFT model to complete.

1. Using a timeline

On a blank piece of paper ask your career pathfinder to draw a time line from birth to the present day and beyond, with age along the horizontal axis and happiness along the vertical axis. When complete, the time line should look something like the diagram below, with highs and lows throughout a person's life. When they get to the present day encourage them to consider what they hope or expect the future to hold.

Timelines can reveal many aspects of a person's life, whether inside or outside of work. They should include important facts, such as deaths, (if married) wedding day, divorce, births. This gives you more background data of which to be aware when helping them discern their career path.

Asking your pathfinder to draw what they hope and fear in the future can be equally revealing. One client drew a very deep low in the future and after enquiring about this, it became apparent that this reflected his fear of the reality that his father – who was a great inspiration to him – was nearing the end of his life. This type of information can be useful in that it may alter the geography of where your pathfinder may look for work.

Another client may be considering starting a family in the future. If this is the case, they may need to consider how they will combine childcare and work in the new role, which may affect the location of workplace, home and childcare provision.

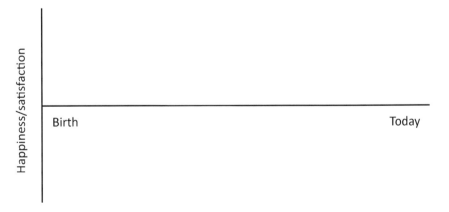

Once the timeline is complete, arm yourself with lots of sticky notes, and ask your pathfinder to talk through their time line, exploring the highs and lows (both inside and outside of work), jotting down the skills and experiences, areas of knowledge, and values that may emerge, each one on its own sticky note.

As they tell their story, your main aim is to ask questions to help them talk about the things they loved to do at each stage of their time line. The following questions might be helpful at different stages along the timeline:

During primary school

- What skills did you learn from your parents?
- What were your favourite subjects at school?
- What activities or projects did you get involved with outside school that you loved?
- When there was nothing else to do, how did you occupy yourself?

During secondary school

- What were your favourite subjects at school?
- What activities and projects did you get involved with outside school that you loved?
- What positions of responsibility were you given? What skills were you using here?

During college or university

- What were your favourite subjects at college/university?
- What activities and projects did you get involved with outside your course that you loved?
- What clubs did you join?
- What positions of responsibility were you given? What skills were you using here?

Talking through each job role as it would appear on a CV

- What were the skills you were using in each role?
- Which role did you enjoy the most?

- What training courses did you attend on the job? Which were the most enjoyable?
- What subjects have you enjoyed training others in?

At the end of the time line, ask some of these questions

- What subjects do you find yourself reading, talking or thinking about with a passion?
- If funding were available, what area of full-time study would you undertake?
- If money was no object and you did not have to work, what would you actually do to fill the time?

This conversation may take one to two hours, if done in detail. At the end of this time you will have a pile of sticky notes each with one word on it. Some may be skills, others may be areas of knowledge, experiences, or character traits. Keep these to one side whilst you take your pathfinder through the next exercise.

2. Using pictures

Now ask your pathfinder to draw three situations (inside or outside of work) where they achieved a 'yes' factor of satisfaction. Stick people are fine, you do not need to be an artist for this exercise. This exercise helps your pathfinder to connect with the emotional aspects of the different situations, by using a different part of their brain.

Some people find this exercise challenging. Reassure them that it is purely an exercise, no artistic ability is required, and go with the first situations that come to mind without thinking too much. If this exercise really proves unhelpful, abandon it.

Assuming your pathfinder is happy to proceed, ask them to talk about each scenario, whilst you ask probing questions:

- What skills were you using in each situation?
- What are the themes that link each of the pictures?
- How do these pictures inform you about your future career?

As your pathfinder talks, add any more skills experience and knowledge to your pile of sticky notes as they surface. Do not worry if you have duplicated any from before. Now ask your pathfinder to look down the skills list earlier in the book. Which of these skills do they absolutely love? Add them to separate sticky notes and combine them with the others you already have.

Now ask your pathfinder to take time to complete the steps in 'Compiling your Top 10 skills' starting at point 5 above, arriving at your next session with the Top 10 skills in priority order.

⑪– Defining your Heart, your passion and purpose at work

The next stage of the process is to define your Heart, your passion and purpose at work. Answer these questions with the first thing that comes into your mind. You can do this exercise alone, but having a career guide to ask you the questions allows you to think unhindered, while they write down the values and themes that emerge.

> *The thing that makes me most angry – and that I most want to put right in the world is...*
>
> *I dream about...*
>
> *My energy and passion at work lies...*
>
> *I close down at work when...*
>
> *At my very best, I am...*
>
> *At work I make a stand for...*
>
> *What I really, really want is...*

From these statements and from the themes and values, which may have arisen from your House of Life or Time Line, complete the following sentences:

- The values that really matter to me in my work are...

- My main purpose in all the work I do is to...

Add a summary of your passions and values to the Heart section of your SHIFT diagram.

Sarah (Chapter 2) discerned from her Top 10 skills that she loved coaching and facilitation and could do it very well. As she went on in her career she had some bad experiences with leadership and management and on reflection realised the thing she was most passionate about was leading and managing others well and empowering them. This became her heart's passion more than coaching and facilitation and this is what she cannot stop herself from doing. She now runs a charity with fifty people and achieved a 97% work satisfaction score just recently. She is also coaching and advising other charities about leadership and management.

In my experience, when you work from your heart, success follows, as you are doing what comes naturally to you.

F – Identifying Fears, assumptions and blocks to action

Part 1[ix]

You want to make some changes to your career yet at the same time you probably have some fears, negative beliefs and doubts that hold you back from action. What assumptions are holding you back? What is your inner 'voice' telling you that stops you from taking action?

Read the checklist opposite of some common barriers and constraints to change. Circle any that ring true for you.

If you are using a career guide, explore some of these barriers or assumptions. As you explore them, you might find that the blocks do not seem as solid as they were when you first thought of them, and they might gradually begin to disappear. Other blocks may be real and unchangeable and something else has to move them from your path.

Sarah (Chapter 2) had to leave her old workplace and was offered two jobs, one with a firm salary and organisational structure and another that was a start-up scenario with no structure, and questionable salary. Having just got a mortgage, everything seemed to point to the safer job, although her heart was in the start-up company. Her mortgage was becoming a block to action until the head of the start-up company set up a board of trustees and found funding for her salary in the space of two days. Many things are possible when you explore the blocks, stick to your heart, and see how you can get round the blocks, sometimes with a little help from your friends.

My job search to date hasn't worked well	I am under-qualified	My experience is all in one industry	Travel to work distance	Travel as part of job
Nights away from home	Lack of information about the job market	The stigma of unemployment	No clear career goals	Financial commitments
Family/ personal problems	I want a safe job	Few measurable achievements	Attitudes/ needs of family members	Lack of confidence in selling myself in person
Worry that I will repeat old problems	Lack of up-to-date skills	Worry that I will be out of work for a long time	Worry about taking risks	I don't have time
Fear of failure	I have health problems	Fear of rejection	Lack of relevant qualifications	I am too old
I have lots of ideas but struggle to act on them	I don't interview well	I have never had to apply for a job before	Lack of up-to-date knowledge	I am out of touch with the job market
Don't want to make the rong decision at this stage of my life	I expect the HR / the company to manage my career	Worry about having to retrain / go back to full time study	Want to get a job that looks good on my CV	Fear of employers' attitude to redundancy or unemployment
I'm not good enough	I am not a finisher	Fear of approaching people	If it's not hard or difficult how can it be growing me?	?

Part 2ˣ

It's worth taking a clear look at both the positive forces that are driving change and the negative forces that might be holding you back, as we considered in Part 1 above. Make some notes around the diagram below with this in mind:

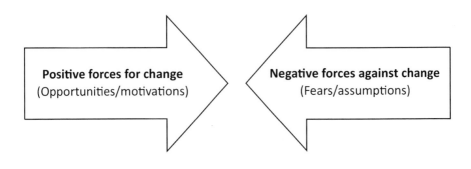

Positive forces for change
(Opportunities/motivations)

Negative forces against change
(Fears/assumptions)

The following questions can be answered on your own or with your career guide.

1. Barriers and constraints are sometimes concrete, but often they are strategies for avoiding taking action and making change happen. What are your favourite 'Yes, but...' defences?

2. How can you overcome some of these 'Yes, but...' statements or negative forces?

Add a summary of your fears or 'barriers to change' on your SHIFT model.

T – defining Traits and type of personality

Your strongest personal traits

1. Overleaf is a Traits questionnaire[xi] for you to photocopy and pass on to five friends and colleagues. Complete one yourself before you look at the other results, so it is not skewed by their feedback

2. Ask your friends and colleagues to tick as many traits that they observe in you, marking your top three.

3. Once you have received the forms back, collate the answers so that you form a list

   ❑ Traits that all five people have observed.

   ❑ Traits that four people have observed.

   ❑ Traits that three people have observed.

   ❑ Traits that two people have observed.

   ❑ Traits that an individual have observed.

4. Compare your own answers with your results. What surprises you?

5. Write your Top 10 strongest traits here and onto the SHIFT model (on page 46).

1)   6)

2)   7)

3)   8)

4)   9)

5)   10)

Results from this exercise should help you to define the traits that you take to any role you do (i.e. those which all five people see) and will also give you the right information to answer an interview question such as 'What type of person would your friends/colleagues say you are?'

DISCOVERING YOUR PERSONAL TRAITS

Feedback for: ....

Feedback from: ....

Date to be returned:...

For the person named above, please tick as many of the following traits that you observe to be their strongest, and highlight their top three. Please return this form to them by the date indicated above.

The information used will be collated with feedback from others and used for career direction purposes.

- Accurate
- Achievement orientated
- Adaptable
- Adept
- Adventurous
- Alert
- Appreciative
- Assertive
- Astute
- Authoritative
- Calm
- Cautious
- Charismatic
- Competent
- Consistent
- Contagiously enthusiastic
- Co-operative
- Courageous
- Creative
- Decisive
- Deliberate
- Dependable
- Diligent
- Diplomatic

- Discreet
- Driving
- Dynamic
- Extremely economical
- Effective
- Energetic
- Enthusiastic
- Experienced
- Expert
- Firm
- Flexible
- Fun
- Impulsive
- Independent
- Innovative
- Knowledgeable
- Loyal
- Methodical
- Objective
- Open-minded
- Outgoing
- Outstanding
- Patient
- People-orientated
- Perceptive

- Persevering
- Persistent
- Pioneering
- Practical
- Professional
- Protective
- Punctual
- Quick/works quickly
- Rational
- Realistic
- Reliable
- Resourceful
- Responsible
- Responsive
- Safeguarding
- Self-motivated
- Self reliant
- Sensitive
- Sophisticated
- Strong
- Supportive
- Tactful
- Thorough
- Unique
- Versatile
- Vigorous

Your type of personality or preferences

One of the most useful tools I have used with clients to help them understand their inherent preferences – and therefore the career path that is most suited to their type – is the Myers Briggs Type Indicator (MBTI).

The MBTI is a self-report questionnaire, which is designed to make Jung's theory of psychological types more understandable for everyday life. It describes a person's preference in four spectrums:

- Extroversion and Introversion – how you gain your energy either from being with a lot of people or being alone;

- Sensing and Intuition – how you gather data and information either from what you sense through seeing, hearing, touching and so on, or from seeing pictures and patterns in the data;

- Thinking and Feeling – how you make decisions using either your rational thinking process or your feelings;

- Judging and Perceiving – how you make sense of the world either by structure and closure to events or from spontaneity and leaving possibilities to the last minute.

To understand a little of what a preference is, write your signature on a piece of paper with your preferred hand, as you would normally do. Now write your signature with your other hand. What did it feel like? Most people who do this exercise find that writing with their non-preferred hand feels unnatural, awkward and clumsy, and that they had to concentrate to do it.

One of my clients broke her arm and while it was in plaster she became very skilled at writing with her non-preferred hand. So, whilst we have a natural preference (in this case left- or right-handedness), we can learn to do the opposite preference. Indeed, for effective careers we need to learn to be flexible and operate often from our non-preferred preferences. So this is also the case with Jung's preferences. There is one that we naturally do and the opposite preference we can do but have to learn to do over time to be really effective, or find others with the preferences we do not have to make a good team.

Completing a questionnaire

I do not intend to go into more detail about MBTI as there is a wealth of published material online about it if you wish to learn more. To complete a questionnaire, which will discern your MBTI 'type', the ideal scenario is to find an MBTI-qualified coach to administer it and take you through what the results mean for you in your career. Qualified practitioners can provide a specific MBTI report relevant to careers. If you choose this route visit my website or get in touch with one of my coaches and we can put you in touch with trained practitioners.

An alternative and cheaper route is to complete one of the free online MBTI questionnaires, for example *www.truity.com/test/type-finder-research-edition*. Once completed it will tell you your MBTI type and provide a link to typical careers suitable for people with your type. As a warning though, several people I know have used this method and have ended up with the links to unsuitable choices. Sometimes when we complete online questionnaires we answer the questions with our 'work brain' or learnt preferences rather than our natural ones, largely because we have become very practised at writing with our 'opposite' hand. At times, we can also answer them with conditioned responses around what we think we should be or want to be, rather than who we truly are. Finding the type that best fits you is the aim of the MBTI practitioner, which may be worth investing in.

If you take MBTI, summarise the information from your MBTI report about your preferences and add it to your SHIFT checklist. You will probably notice that some of the traits that your friends and colleagues have observed in you may also show up in your MBTI report. Notice the duplications and record or underline these. From the careers typical for your MBTI type, which interest you? Write these on the role section of the Environment 'grid', that I will explore in more detail later in the book.

In summary

You should now have a completed grid, including all the checklists that emerged from working through the SHIFT model. This is how you see things at this moment, but of course as you understand yourself better you will be able to refine this chart. Don't see it as set in stone, but rather a working document that you will return to and refine over the years to come. SHIFT is the first part of your discernment process, we now turn to the second: your ideal working environment.

Chapter 4

EXPLORING YOUR IDEAL WORKING ENVIRONMENT

For the moment, forget about your organisation's structure and your current job title. Answer the questions overleaf to build a picture of your ideal work environment and add a summary of your comments to your environment grid diagram below.

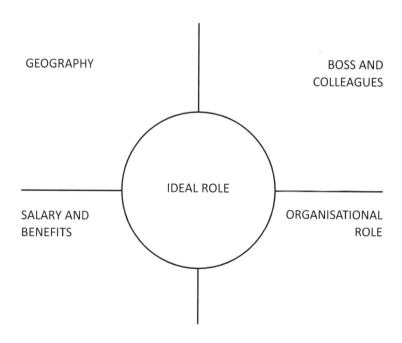

1. Role

What sorts of roles would you consider now, based on all that emerged from the SHIFT process? Brainstorm these with your career guide, if you have one, or show your diagram to your friends and family and ask their advice.

- What roles have you found exciting and engaging in the past?
- What appeals to you in other people's roles?
- Which roles surfaced in your MBTI report that are of interest to you?

2. Your ideal line manager and colleagues

A growing body of evidence shows that as many as 70% of employees are unhappy at work and more often than not a line manager has a huge part to play in this[xii.] When you go to an interview, remember you are interviewing them as much as they are interviewing you.

One client I worked for figured out his SHIFT profile and realised he was in the right job in the right company although his boss made his life an absolute misery. Fortunately his boss left and he began to thrive in his role under a new boss, rather than being stifled and stressed. The organisation was close to losing a very skilled operator who later became a Senior Vice President.

Your ideal line manager

On a blank piece of paper:

- Draw (stick people are fine) the best boss you have ever worked for.
- What are the attributes that you valued most in this boss? Label them on your drawing.
- Now draw the worst boss you have ever worked for.
- What are the attributes that you most disliked in this boss? Label them on your drawing.
- On this second drawing, reverse the attributes that you hated most e.g., 'was so task-focused' could be reversed to 'so team-focused'.
- From both drawings, discern the qualities that you would like to see in your future boss and write these in priority order on your environment diagram.

- When going for interview, use this list when meeting your new boss and ask questions that will help you to understand his/her leadership style. If possible find out more information from existing colleagues working for them.

Your colleagues

If it is helpful, repeat the steps above in working out your ideal line manager. Instead use the teams you have worked with as the centre of your drawing or answer the following:

- What kinds of people do you **most** and **least** enjoy working with?
- Do you enjoy leading and managing others? How many?
- Do you prefer customer interaction or working internally?
- How many people do you like working with in a team?
- How many people is the ideal number for the total organisation?

Add a summary of your findings to the Environment grid.

If possible, once you have been offered a new job, ask if you can spend a day with the new organisation before accepting the offer. Before I accepted the research role for a grocery institute, I spent a day with the people I was going to work for. It was a helpful insight into the culture, type of people and boss that I was going to work for. Its never fail safe, but it does give you more data and confidence that you are making a more informed choice.

3. Geography

Where we work is an important factor in discerning our ideal role. Some would love to work in foreign countries, for others this would be their worst-case scenario.

- Where would you most like to work in the UK?
- If you are attracted to working abroad, what sort of country? Where in the world?
- How long are you prepared to commute to work?
- How would you prefer to travel?
- What are the geographical constrictions, if any? For example aging relatives, partner's work, and children's schools.

Add a summary to your environment grid.

4. Organisational environment

Organisational culture varies enormously from company to company. This is true in the not-for-profit sector as well. So finding an organisational fit is part of the process for finding your dream job.

- What would your ideal organisational culture and environment be like?
- In what kind of organisational culture do you thrive?
- What corporate values are important to you?
- What environments have energised you in the past?
- What sort of physical environment works best for you? (Open plan, own office?)

Add a summary to your environment grid.

5. Salary and benefits

We all have a certain level of salary at which we feel comfortable, and in different seasons of our life there may be particular benefits that interest us.

- Thinking realistically, what is your ideal salary? What do you think you are worth?
- What is the minimum that you or your family could survive on? Work this out in detail so that you know your absolute minimum.
- What benefits do you really need?

Add a summary to your environment grid.

In summary

You have now completed your SHIFT and ideal environment charts – well done!

If you are single, as I was, working through the SHIFT process and then actively pursing it has fewer restrictions. If you are married, have a partner and possibly a family, this whole process needs to be done in consultation with them, so now may be the time to share the insights you have gained so far. Listen carefully to any reflections they have, and recognise that, especially with your partner, they may benefit from doing a similar process so that you can together discern what the next steps might be for both of you.

Chapter 5

CHANGING JOBS

Job-hunting and job-filling strategies[xiii]

Many, if not most, employers fill vacancies in the exact opposite way from how most people search for new jobs. Most jobs are snapped up by those who are clear about what they want and who know the right people to help them get there. With this in mind, think about the top three tiers in the diagram overleaf – how might you reduce the level of risk for a prospective employer?

Your network

Now that you are clear about the ideal role you are working towards and your ideal working environment remember it is whom we know that is more likely to get us our next job. Therefore, begin to think about:

- Who is doing the job you most want?

- Who is working in the organisation or industry you most want to work in?

- Who do your friends or colleagues know who work in these roles/ sectors?

How Employers Typically Prefer to Fill Vacancies:

From within: Promotion of a full-time employee, or promotion of a present part-time employee, or hiring a former consultant for in-house or contract work, or hiring a former 'temp' full-time. Employer's thought 'I want to hire someone whose work I have already seen' (A low-risk-strategy for the employer)

Implication for job-hunters: See if you can get hired at an organisation you have chosen – as a temp, contract worker, or consultant – aiming at a full-time position only later (or not at all)

Using proof: hiring an unknown job-hunter who brings proof of what he or she can do, with regards to the skills needed.

Implication for job-hunters: If you are a Programmer, bring a program you have done - with its code; if you are a photographer, bring photos, if you are a counsellor, bring a case study with you etc

Using a best friend or business colleague: Hiring someone whose work a trusted friend has seen (perhaps they worked for him or her)

Implication for job hunters: Find someone who knows the peson-who-has-the-power-to-hire at your target organisation, who also knows your work and will introduce you two

Using an agency they trust: This may be a recruiter or search firm the employer has hired, or a private employment agency – both of which have checked you out, on behalf of the employer

Using an ad they have placed:
(online or in newspapers etc)

Using a CV: Even if the CV was unsolicited (if the employer is desperate)

How a Job-Hunter Typically Prefers to Job Search

Make a list of all the people you can ask to take out for a 30-minute coffee. Meeting face-to-face, if possible, is essential to building connections. If the page is still blank after a few minutes, ask some close family and friends.

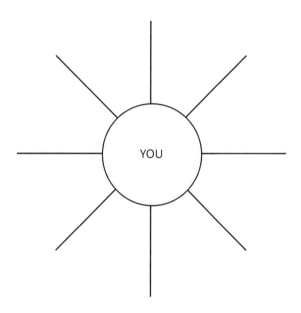

Connecting with others

For those of you who hate networking, remember:

- Most people are willing to help and if they are not, then they are not worth connecting with in the first place.

- It is essential that you meet face-to-face, no excuses.

- A large percentage of jobs are achieved through people who know you or at least have met you.

It is not an option to not network. If you have some blocks to meeting up with strangers, talk this through with your career guide or close friend and seek the support you need to make this possible.

What is your first step to connecting with others?

Questions to ask when networking

When meeting people who are in the industry or role that you want to work in, ask some of the following questions to broaden your understanding:

- How did you get into this work?

- What do you like most about it?

- What do you like least about it?

- What specific skills or experience do you need for this type of work?

- Talk about your SHIFT profile. How does this fit this role and/or environment?

- What do you like/dislike about the culture within the organisation/ industry?

- Who else do they know that you could network with?

When I met Victoria Cassells for the first time, she was then working in the ideal role I wanted, so I was keen to ask her questions about the organisation for which she was working at the time. The information really confirmed what I'd discovered about myself through the SHIFT model, but the environment of the organisation was very cut-throat and target-driven, to the point of exhaustion.

So my journey continued, having discovered my ideal role, to discover the environment or organisation in which I would thrive. As I kept networking, I found a coaching and facilitation organisation that had a better fit with my ideal environment by networking with the father of my vicar.

Networking is not only a form of research; it is also an advert that you are available for work. Sharing your SHIFT profile with prospective employers gives them a clear idea of who you are and what you are looking for, such that if a job does come up or they see an advert for a new role, they may get in touch with you. When I was stuck in my Unilever marketing role, I had completed my SHIIFT profile and shared this with a good friend, Hilary. It was Hilary who saw the advert for my next job and encouraged me to apply.

Applying for new jobs

Now that you are clear about whom you are and where you want to work, it might be that you do not have enough skills and experience to walk straight into your new role or industry just yet. As I've mentioned before, it took me several job changes and eight years of growing my skills and experience to be credible to do the work that Victoria did. For others, it does not take quite so long. However, each time I took a new role or job, I referred to my SHIFT checklist to confirm that I was growing more skills or knowledge to make my vision a reality. As I had sought work that harnessed my passions and was true to what was at the core of me, the criteria did not change over time – a bit like a stick of rock that has the same message running through its centre regardless of where you cut the rock.

In Chapter 1 I introduced the step-change diagram. Refer to this and either try to stay in the same industry but change your role, or move industries and stick to the same role, before you move to a new role and a new industry.

Sarah (Chapter 2) had worked out her SHIFT diagram and knew that coaching and facilitation was what she also wanted to do. However, she had no evidence to prove to a new employer that she was any good at it. She therefore did two step changes – first to a role where her employers needed her for her account management skills and where she could learn coaching and facilitation skills at the same time. The second step change was to set up her charity, her ideal leadership role.

However, some people do manage to move down the very difficult path of changing industries and roles all at the same time.

Peter (chapter 6) was a successful IT consultant who had a passion for helping dyslexic children, having been dyslexic himself and having three dyslexic children of his own. When I started working with him, he and his wife had already started to home school their children, having become frustrated with the education system.

Through exploring his SHIFT diagram and particularly his barriers to setting up a school for dyslexic children – his passion and vision – he slowly gained the support he needed to follow the difficult path and start the school, in London, which is now thriving with over 100 pupils. This example is, however, unusual unless you are setting up a new venture and you can shape the new set-up to meet your needs, with nothing to prove to a new employer.

The curriculum vitae

I am not going to explore how to write a CV, as there are plenty of resources online that will guide you through this process. However, CVs work at their best when they are a follow-up to having met someone within the organisation to which you are applying. Where possible send your CV to the people you have networked with as a follow-up email, in case they hear of a suitable role.

The most successful CVs, in my opinion, take up no more than two sides of A4 paper. The first page lists the skills and experience relevant to the role for which you are applying. The second page contains the chronology of your training and employment. If you are not applying for a particular role, the first page could list some aspects of your SHIFT diagram, which would show a prospective employee who you are.

A client of mine asked me if he should pay a professional to help him write his CV as he had never written one before, having worked mainly for one company. My advice was to write out a two-page version, as above, and get a friend in the industry that he was interested in to check it through and adapt it.

A CV is really just back-up data for people once they have met you. By all means spend time on getting this to the best standard you can, adapting it each time you apply for a different role. However, save your money and spend it on networking with people – far more effective.

Nothing is wasted

Throughout my own career, I have come to use all aspects of the skills, experience and knowledge that I picked up at each stage. Nothing is ever wasted, even the most dreadful or painful parts.

In one organisation I worked for, the chief executive was a real driver for success, often born out of her own insecurity, in my opinion. The upside of this leadership style was that she got results and she transformed a sleepy organisation with a turnover of £1m to £5m in very little time. The downside of this style was that some of the team working for her were ruled by fear and experienced stress and burnout. The culture in the organisation was toxic. I was one of the team members who went off sick with burnout (see Chapter 6). However, from this experience I learned:

- How to deal with people who have a very different leadership style to my own.
- The type of boss for whom I will never work again.
- The type of culture in which I will never work again.
- A case study to use when teaching teams about their different leadership styles.

All experiences can be used as you work towards your new role. The timing of reaching is irrelevant. It will happen if you continue to pursue your vision, knowing that each step of the way you are getting closer towards your goal by learning more skills, experience and knowledge, which will make you credible. Keep remembering that nothing is wasted. The journey may take you down some blind alleys where you learn something you wouldn't have otherwise known.

Part 3

THE **CHALLENGES**

Chapter 6
ILLNESS

People have different approaches to managing illness or injury and their career. There is no one right approach, just the approach that best suits you and supports your wellbeing. In this chapter, I will explain how I managed my career after both physical and mental illness as a result of cancer, as well as how I have had to adapt my career to my new physical limitations. I have also documented case studies of people, all of whom I have worked with, who have successfully managed their careers in spite of their illness or injury.

Physical illness or injury

Having been an executive coach and trainer in business for over ten years, I loved what I was doing, and had SHIFTed my career and worked within school hours as much as possible, for the sake of our sons. I was appreciated, respected and well paid for what I was doing.

In 2011, I was diagnosed with breast cancer, Grade 4, one of the most aggressive types and I had quite a large tumour; how did I miss it for so long? It was like a bombshell. Only four months earlier Rob had been made redundant from his work of 15 years. We had just sold our house but were unable to find the right one to buy so were renting.

Although Rob was beginning to progress his photography business, with the cancer diagnosis, financially it felt rather hairy. We had the reserves of the house sale in the bank but that was to buy our next house. How were we going to keep on generating an income?

The uncertainty of finances on top of a life-limiting diagnosis just seems unfair and yet it is so common. Amazingly for us, the executive coaching group I was affiliated with for the past ten years gave us £5000 unconditionally to keep us afloat. Rob managed to get his new company underway in spite of the tensions at home. I have so much admiration for him considering the pressure he was under.

Whilst I had to drop my training day clients, I managed to keep on my individual clients throughout chemotherapy at least. Amazingly the finances took care of themselves through different means and I have now come to trust that finances will sort themselves out through all sorts of ways however grim it might seem on the outside. Working during the chemotherapy was the only way for me to stay sane. I informed my clients of my treatment as my hair was likely to fall out and it would be obvious. As I reacted quite badly to the chemotherapy, I was only fit to work every third week, however with coaching clients to be seen every 3-4 weeks, I could plan my coaching sessions around my chemotherapy. For me, work symbolised normality and it was a way of me retaining a sense of self, identifying with something I was good at and was part of my identity, away from 'Lorraine the breast cancer patient'.

Other cancer patients I have spoken to have similarly found work to be helpful in coping with treatment. Aisha is an actress, mother of two boys and to pay the bills (or when she is 'resting' from acting) she works as a receptionist. Throughout her radiotherapy she insisted that her treatment was given to her in the mornings so that she could work in the afternoons and carry on life as normal.

Whilst I had passed many of my one-day workshop training clients to my associate colleagues, I wanted to retain one client who I had worked with for seven years and I was due to complete a series of training workshops with the leadership team. Although I had told the leader I was undergoing treatment, we decided not to tell the team at that stage so as not to detract in any way from the workshop. By this time in my treatment, although it was the third week of my chemotherapy cycle, I was beginning to get extremely tired and was not sure I could handle a full workshop alone. I addressed this by asking a good friend and colleague of mine to work alongside me and subsequently look after the client in my absence.

Being freelance and running your own business is a tricky thing when you are struck down with illness. I had no insurance to cover loss of earnings and no direct employer or employees to hand my work over to. However, the flip side is that you gain the freedom to choose your hours, choose who you work for and who you work alongside. I have many very long-standing and trusted professional colleagues within my network and it was these people I turned to for support and wisdom on how should I inform clients. What was manageable now? Who could cover the needs of my clients in my absence and return them to me when I was fit enough to work again?

At the end of chemotherapy, I experienced a very deep 'low' (see the later section on managing mental illness and work), which is quite common amongst cancer patients. I therefore had to stop work altogether and take about four to five months off. I really thought at the time that was the end of my career and I was never going to work again. The love and patience of my family, friends and church got me through this phase. I lost all confidence in ever working again or why anyone would want to pay me now. I was slowly being defined more and more as 'Lorraine, the breast cancer patient' and being able to be normal again seemed almost impossible.

To ease myself back into the vague possibility that I might work again, I went on one or two personal development workshops where I could be 'Lorraine, the executive coach'. I began to engage in 'cappuccino conversations', as we call them, with past clients with no agenda other than to connect and find out how they were doing.

I also decided to make use of my experience and ran a free workshop for a personal development group entitled 'What can illness and/or injury, teach us and how can we use the experiences positively for our lives inside and outside work?' Other than helping others explore their own issues, this was a chance for me to get back in the saddle once again. This was so successful that I ran a similar workshop for one of my corporate clients, and of all the workshops I have run, this is the one that achieved the feedback equivalent of a standing ovation.

Slowly I could see that work was possible once again and all credit to my associate colleagues, every single client I had handed over to them almost six to eight months previously, came back to me of their own volition. I was back in business again. I continued building my business and it became so successful that I eventually set up my own limited company, earning far more money than I had ever done before. This was only possible with Rob's support as we worked out a way of us both working flexibly and sharing the childcare between us.

After three years, we finally moved from our rented house. For me, this move was about creating safety for the family in a very unsafe and uncertain situation where the cancer could return at any stage. One of the models I use in my work is 'Towards a position of safe uncertainty'.

Towards a position of safe uncertainty

Our house move provides an illustration of how to use the diagram below. Having cancer felt very uncertain, and at the same time felt very unsafe as we were not in a permanent home, my eldest son had to move from a primary to a secondary school, and Rob no longer had a studio for his work due to his redundancy. We knew we needed to move to a place of safe uncertainty.

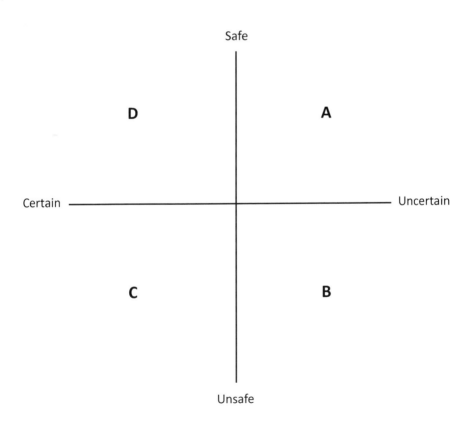

We therefore decided to find a house, which had:

- One of the best cancer hospitals within 10 minutes drive.

- Good primary and secondary schools within walking distance.

- The ability to make a studio for Rob and a study for me.

- Fields at the back for dog walks and general sanity.

- A good local church within walking distance.

We created safety as much as we could to enable the family to be as independent as possible even though we lived with the uncertainty that the cancer could return.

In January 2014, I reset my password for my work emails as 'Freedom 2014'. Whilst the move had been tough for many reasons, work was flying and I really felt as though things were on the up. Free at last, but not for long. In April 2014, after a month of pain, dizziness and sickness, I was told I had secondary breast cancer that had formed a tumour in my cerebellum. The tumour was the size of a golf ball and needed urgent surgery if I was to survive.

In the safe uncertainty model, I was now in Box C. There was certainty that the cancer had returned and hope of a complete cure, medically, was now out of the question.

Having been through the mastectomy, I naively thought I would bounce back in a few months. Even the night before the surgery I was writing notes and briefing my supervisor with all the necessary details of running my clients in my absence. I think I was blissfully in denial whilst my family was wondering if I would actually make it through the operation.

If the tumour remained in my head, there was the certainty that death would follow. Death (and life after it, if you believe what the Bible says) is the only certainty in this life, if you think about it (Box D). Surgery thankfully was successful but now I was in Box B. The future was very uncertain and it also felt very unsafe.

After nine weeks in various hospitals and hospices, I was quite disabled with double vision, inability to walk, slurred speech, shot balance and dizziness and motion sickness, which meant every time I moved my head I was sick. I was not in a good way.

Months of physiotherapy, hospital scans, therapeutic interventions, visits from friends and family ensued and it became a bit like a merry-go-round. The kindness of friends and family both locally and on the end of the phone was just amazing. Meals were made for several weeks, trips to hospital, help with the boys' activities, lawn-mowing, shopping, and so many cards with lovely encouraging words.

Bit by bit, the symptoms diminished sufficiently for me to function better at home. I was beginning to move to Box A ever so gradually. One year later I finally got my driving licence back, which made a world of difference to my independence. I was extremely fatigued and the prospect of work seemed impossible. However because my one-to-one coaching work actually gave me energy, I found ways of coaching friends for free on issues they were facing, on the understanding that I could cancel at any time if I was not up to it. I was still able to be effective sitting down, in spite of my disabilities.

I then began to think of what I could manage given my disability. My face-to-face coaching sessions were usually two hours long, which did not seem manageable now. All my clients were based in London for large corporations. My extreme fatigue meant travelling into London for work was no longer an option.

I decided to write (hence this book) because I could pick it up and put it down whenever it suited me. A new career-coaching client was also referred to me and we began coaching for free for the first three sessions whilst we figured out the best conference-calling medium to work with. These sessions lasted 90 minutes, were based from my study, required no travel time and were very manageable from a fatigue point of view. Although, as they were free, I could also have the liberty of cancelling if I was too unwell or tired before the session. The joy of working again from my revised SHIFT pattern gave me a renewed sense of purpose and energy.

I also found myself able to support Rob's photography business, Purpix Photography, when I felt up to it. I used to be a marketing manager at Unilever (although I never regarded these skills as 'skills I loved'), so I began to use these skills for the marketing and PR for his work.

Through networking, I helped him become the local magazine photographer, wrote PR articles, produced leaflets for his photography courses as well as created his wall of fame of people's testimonies. Again, this was something that I could pick up and put down again if I was too fatigued.

Rob is an 'easy sell' as he is working from his own gifting, having worked as a film director/producer as well as a photographer. He is extremely gifted in telling stories through still or moving pictures. He is a true artist and he loves communicating through pictures. He has made his hobby, which began as an eight-year-old boy with a new camera, into a career that pays.

With this new focus on writing books, coaching via the Internet and supporting Rob where I could, I regained a new calling for the next season, other than my primary calling as a wife and mother of two gorgeous boys. From my new SHIFT profile, I am still using my Top 5 skills whether in the home or through the work, as well as some other skills that were present but not necessarily in my Top 10.

Lessons from my story

Here are some reflections from my story to apply to your own career journey:

- Work out your SHIFT profile and do it as soon as you can; you don't need to wait for work to get really bad or illness to strike. It will give you a fresh perspective and renewed purpose.

- In my experience, during this time and other times, I have learned to trust finances will sort themselves out, often in unexpected ways.

- Working through treatment can be a good way to stay sane and maintain normality.

- Make sure you have an understanding employer or network of professional colleagues around you. Get all the support you can from them.

- Re-engage in work in a very low-key way. Just meeting colleagues for coffee or doing a bit of work for free to gain your confidence.

- Use your experience to help others facing a similar situation – it helps to make sense of it all and can be quite therapeutic.

- Trust that all things are possible. Working again for me seemed so unlikely, but I have managed to return to work.

Others' stories

The following two case studies are people I have worked with: Jane who suffered physical injury as a result of a car crash and Susie who, like me, is re-defining her career after the onslaught of cancer. Having been through the cancer journey myself, it was a pure joy to work with Susie, in particular as somehow I had gone before her and could use my horrible experience, coupled with my work experience in a much deeper way. Whatever physical illness you or someone you are supporting are facing, I hope you discover something new from these stories to support you.

Story 1: Jane

I was on skiing holiday and when we were driving back from the slopes I had a head-on collision with another car. I was 26. I fractured my back and had crushed several vertebrae, broke my nose as I hit the windscreen and had numerous cuts all over my face. I went to hospital to be stitched up which even involved stitching my eyelids. It was a nightmare!

At the time I was working for an insurance company in sales and credit underwriting. I had stayed with my parents to recover, although our family motto is 'just get back up and keep going'. So two weeks later I was back to work. Colleagues were shocked I came back so early. There was no support offered to ease me back into work, I just got on with it and returned to normal, except things weren't normal.

I remember walking in a car park with a work colleague when a car screeched round a corner. I must have flinched in such a way to cause him to ask if I was all right and whether I got nightmares about the accident. I was numb and operating on autopilot most of the time. Post-traumatic stress nightmares stayed with me for about ten years.

In hindsight I should have taken more time off work and I know work would have agreed. It just seemed the best idea to try and return to normal, as I was not getting much comfort from being with my parents and I needed to be distracted. Ideally it would have helped to talk through the trauma or join a group of people who had suffered similar injuries. What was going on inside me was in such contrast to what people were seeing on the outside.

Going back to work too soon meant that I was still dealing with the trauma ten years later. To help me grieve, I handed in my notice and undertook postgraduate studies to be able to leave that chapter in my life behind.

Lessons from Jane's story

Here are some reflections from Jane's story to apply to your own career journey:

- Take more time off than you need or think you need, it will save you emotional pain in the long term.
- Find a therapist to talk through the trauma.
- Find a group of fellow suffers if you can or connect with people you know who have had a similar experience.
- Find a way of 'ending' that chapter and moving onto another chapter.

Story 2: Andy

As a lawyer I was making a name for myself in international law and international relations. I was regularly asked to attend conferences to address human-rights issues globally. I was using my skills and talent to make a difference to the lives of people around the world. If I were to rate my job it would have been 11/10.

In 2010 I was diagnosed with bowl cancer. The biopsy results confirmed I had an aggressive cancer and I had an operation to remove some of my bowl. The biggest challenge for me was going from being independent and successful in my job to feeling overwhelmed and uncertain after my diagnosis. I had to get my strength back but also find a new way of being confident in my ability to work.

Before and after my operation work were supportive but six months later my role in the firm was made redundant. It was extremely traumatic to be in recovery and looking for a new job. Cancer had taken away a great deal of my confidence and my ability to think straight had really been impaired. I think this was a combination of the effect of the treatment but also my response to the shock and trauma of facing a serious illness. I was living off my savings and I knew I had to get a job. But I was really worried how a prospective employer would view me.

I applied for a position in a slightly different legal field and was successful in getting the job. I was very nervous about telling my new employer about my cancer. But once I had I was amazed at how supportive the company was.

They had policies and procedures in place for a number of life issues that might affect their employees. They helped me talk through my concerns and consider the hours and breaks that I needed. I really found follow up hospital appointments stressful, but it made all the difference having line managers who were really supportive, giving me flexibility to go to them. They also had a gym and subsidized treatments such as massage therapy.

Work became a source of pride for me and helped me see that I was able to work again. Wow! What a difference a good line manager and thought through HR policies can make to employees getting back to work after a serious illness.

There were a number of other things that helped me get back to work and stay working:

- *Support from friends and family.*
- *One friend cooked a meal for me once a week.*
- *Online grocery shopping.*
- *Going to bed by 8pm each night, as energy levels were knocked. My sleeping patterns got back to normal over a year.*
- *Swimming regularly.*
- *Getting back into running once I was able to post-treatment.*

My advice to anyone recovering from any serious illness is to take time out and reflect on:

- *What has changed?*
- *What you fear has changed versus what has actually changed.*
- *Keep a log of your recovery – ask yourself what can you do that you couldn't do a month ago – things might be really bad now but you will get stronger – and what you can do will change with time – be easy on yourself and allow yourself time to recuperate.*
- *If you are worried about not being able to do everything you want to do in life, make a list of the priorities and see if you can do them.*
- *Serious illnesses create a number of challenges physical, emotional and mental. There were specific things I hoped to achieve in my life and things in the workplace I thought I had a unique ability to achieve. Things that mattered and made a difference. I found myself asking 'If I have bowl cancer how can I achieve those things?' I would get very angry and frustrated by my situation. This is a natural part of coming to terms with a serious illness. The best thing to do is to get help from someone who can support you through this emotional rollercoaster.*

Ask your GP for recommendations for trained experts who can help you process these thoughts and frustrations and help you develop a new appetite for life in spite of what you have gone through.

Managing transitions

During physical illness

Andy's story reminds me of a useful model by William Bridges in his book *Managing Transitions*[xiv]. Whilst the book is written for businesses managing transitions it is equally applicable for us as we transition from one situation to another.

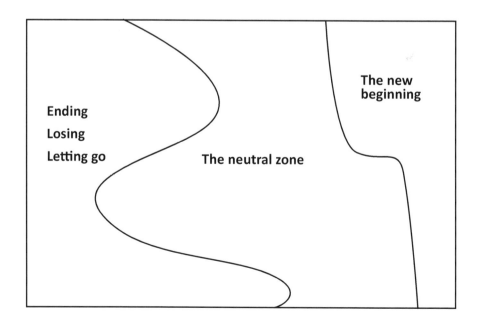

Here is a brief explanation of the model although I would recommend you get the book to understand it further.

Phase 1: Ending, losing, letting go

Once something has come to an end there is a need to Identify what has been lost and who has lost what. In my case initially it was:

- Ability to walk, speak without slurring, double vision, balance.
- Loss of an active driving wife and mother.
- Loss of income.
- Loss of independence.
- Loss of the job I loved that gave me energy.
- Strain on my husband and boys.
- Loss of security for the family with the fear of death hanging over us.

The next step in this phase is to accept the reality and importance of losses. This is a hard one – can I really accept this new phase of life? However it is totally necessary to be able to overcome it and move on to improve and get better. To accept this is how I am now and in a week or a month's time I will be that bit better – is a useful motto. When I first came out of the hospice I had to re-learn to walk and had a walking stick to help me. My boys were mortified at me meeting them at the school gate with a stick, however in a couple of months I had improved sufficiently not to need a stick and now they do not remember me ever using one.

The emotional impact of such huge losses should never be underestimated. The next step is to expect and accept signs of grieving. This may not hit you immediately and can be a delayed reaction as in my case. For the first 18 months post brain tumour my motto of 'keep on keeping on' served me well. When I was in pain unexpectedly for a month with no one able to identify the cause, I just couldn't stop myself crying, not just for the pain but also for the loss of my old healthy life.

The following diagram by Kubler-Ross summarises some of the emotions we go through as we move through to better health. This is the classic bereavement curve and we can get stuck at certain points of the curve unless we seek help.

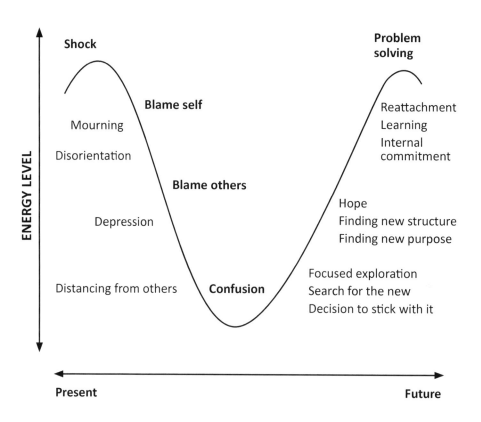

ENERGY LEVEL

Shock

Problem solving

Blame self

Mourning

Reattachment
Learning
Internal commitment

Disorientation

Blame others

Hope
Finding new structure
Finding new purpose

Depression

Distancing from others

Confusion

Focused exploration
Search for the new
Decision to stick with it

Present

Future

The next step of the ending phase is to compensate for the losses. In my case what could I put in place to make sure some of what was lost could be replaced in a different way? Here were some of the things I put in place:

- Online shopping at all times.

- Recruited a driving live-out au pair.

- Recruited three lovely 16-year-old role model boys to come and help when needed.

- Went to Florida and then South Africa for family holidays to give the boys great memories of time together.

- Networked locally and developed a support group.

- Recruited a dog walker when I was not up to the job and Rob was working.

- Started writing to make sense of my work for the last 20 years.

The next step in this phase is to give people information. Everyone handles illness differently and respect individual choices. In my case it was obvious I was very ill as I spent nine weeks in hospital or hospices and my boys came to see me in quite a bad state. What was important for them, I believe, was to let them know what was happening to me with as much information as they needed at that point, and to reassure them that I was not keeping anything from them.

The next step is to define what is over and what is not. To create safety for the family (see the Safe Uncertainty model before), it was important to keep the family doing the same things they were used to doing before, working or going to school, doing the same activities where possible, keeping in touch with friends. Creating safety out of familiarity was the key.

Defining what was over was rather obvious and not something I needed to voice to my family, but for myself it was helpful to consciously recognise the losses: I was no longer able to be so active; I couldn't work in London and lost the income that came with it. However what was not lost was the ability to be there emotionally for the family amidst the rollercoaster of emotions they were experiencing. I was still alive and still a wife and mother with some limitations but emotionally and spiritually stronger as a result.

The final step in this stage is to mark the endings. When it comes to the ending of a team or a project it is easy to celebrate the end with a drink or gathering. In my case I am not sure I officially 'marked the end' of health as I knew it. I did though decide to throw a birthday party for a small group of my closest friends to thank them for carrying me and the family through the worst time of our lives. I was feeling particularly awful at the time so did not feel like an official marking of the ending. However days later I improved radically and a new chapter of better health began for a short while.

Phase 2: The neutral zone

Once we have gone through the 'Ending losing and letting go' phase, the next phase is the neutral zone. This is where the old way of being has passed and a new normal begins to emerge, although it is very embryonic. This can be psychologically a difficult phase as systems and new ways of being are yet to be established. Acknowledging and normalising that this is a difficult phase is half the battle.

This stage requires the need to redefine temporary systems. In my case, involving the boys in helping more around the house with washing, ironing, dishwasher unloading and cooking, and bringing on board external help in the house. I also developed a closer local network of people I could call on if necessary.

Whilst a lot of families struggle with illness and adapting to its impact, it is probably at this stage, like with organisations, that families break up as the strain is too much emotionally. The bond of marriage has remained strong, although it has been extremely tough and something as a family we have all wanted to run away from at times.

Lastly the neutral zone can also be a place of high creativity. When the old has passed away, there is space to begin to think about what is possible in this new phase. Here are some of the things we came up with:

- Coaching on Facetime or Skype rather than coaching in London. I could do an hour working from my office in my pyjamas and manage fatigue levels without the commute.
- Converting our cold conservatory into a creative woodwork workshop – only at the idea stage at the moment.
- Using an electric bike to get me around whilst I was not driving to give me independence but also do something I love – cycling.
- Taking up table tennis, as it was the only ball sport I could play – and beat people at it in the process. It was good to know I had not lost my squash-competitive edge.

Phase 3: The new beginning

This phase is clearly where a new normal takes its shape and there is a new purpose and picture for the future. The picture becomes more clearly defined and a plan develops which brings structure, safety and a sense of direction. Here the different parts that are played by different people become defined and together there is a renewed energy and purpose or calling, which would never have taken place if the old had not passed away. I liken it to the seasons. A magnolia tree which has to lose its leaves in the winter and looks very barren for several months before amazing pure purple flowers emerge bringing a glorious burst of colour and new life.

My new beginning has started for us. Some of it is still unfolding. It involves:

- A renewed focus on the family and the dynamics within it. Equipping them to be as independent and resilient as possible in the face of adversity.

- Defining roles for each member of the family so that the chores are shared more appropriately.

- Supporting Rob's photography business where I can, which at the moment is our sole source of income.

- Writing a book to make sense of my work and personal experience over these past years.

- Continuing my executive coaching work through different media giving hope to reviving my business.

- Helping clients find their own SHIFT path after serious illnesses, given their new limitations to health.

- Writing another book about how my spiritual journey has deepened through this nightmare.

So how does this managing transitions model apply to you? Where are you on the emotional rollercoaster?

During mental illness

Generally speaking, people are more comfortable with the issues surrounding physical illness than they are with mental illness. One in three people suffers from cancer at some time in their life and almost everyone knows someone who has had treatment. Similarly with mental illness: one in four people suffer from mental illness at some point in their lives, yet it's unlikely you'd be aware of it if somebody in your work environment or peer group was struggling with some form of it. Mental illness is often misunderstood, not acknowledged and sometimes seen as a weakness by the uneducated. The following case studies, including my own experience, are a small attempt to normalise this type of illness that affects so many of us. I hope you find it helpful.

Admitting to mental illness is half the battle. Unfortunately there is so much that is misunderstood about mental illness that it is rarely talked about, unless you are Stephen Fry or Robbie Williams, who have used their fame to hopefully educate people and normalise it. With so many people at some point in their life suffering from mental illness, or burnout, which is a more popular and acceptable term in business, we need to take it seriously.

Here I have documented my own experience of recovering from mental illness as a direct result of the cancer treatment. I have also given some case studies of people I have coached back to work who experienced burnout largely from working in the wrong job (not working from their SHIFT profile) or in the wrong environment.

My story

At the end of my chemotherapy treatment I began to notice some of the familiar symptoms of becoming mentally ill (from bouts of illness a long time back brought on by work and exam stress); poor sleep patterns, losing my appetite, losing weight, losing concentration and struggling to make simple decisions, to name a few.

I did not know it at the time, but later found out, that I was hyper-sensitive to steroids that are frequently given to chemotherapy patients. Steroids can cause me to become manic, and if exposed over a longer period, can cause me to become highly depressed to the point of wanting to take my own life.

Having a cancer diagnosis was scary enough, although becoming mentally ill at the end of treatment was far worse for me, and everybody around me. I knew all the coping strategies to help try and manage this onslaught and I was using them all:

- Exercise well.
- Eat well even when you do not feel like it.
- Talk to a therapist.
- Drink lots of chamomile tea.
- Hot baths.
- Lavender oil and candles.
- Check in with doctors.
- Read trashy books or watch trashy films.
- Surround yourself with resourceful people who love you.
- Do things that energise you.
- Sleeping tablets to break the pattern if all else fails.

Yet none of it was working. This was a chemical imbalance in my brain that no amount of coping strategies was going to solve quickly.

When you cannot think straight and all you think about is how you can end your life, there is little hope for life ever being worth living, however long you might have left due to cancer, let alone the thought of working again. I convinced myself that if my business clients knew about this illness they would not want to work with me again. I would think 'People understand and accept cancer, but it is best not to talk about mental illness.'

Again the unconditional support from family and friends who walked with us through this miserable path, sustained us as a family. Slowly I began to stabilise, continuing my coping strategies, although it took a good three to four months before I was dipping my toe in the water work-wise and starting those cappuccino conversations I mentioned earlier.

Lessons from my story

Here are some reflections from my story to apply to your own career journey:

- Mental illness is often caused by a chemical imbalance in the brain, although in this case it was induced by steroids, which is also quite common.
- Chemical imbalances cannot easily be solved by positive thinking or by coping strategies. It takes time to recover.
- Surround yourself with friends and family who love you no matter what.
- Believe that work is possible again even when everything looks bleak.
- Start making small connections with people to reintroduce yourself to the normal world when you are ready.

Story 1: Sajid

I was involved in a big cultural change at work, as a marketing manager, which required the implementation of a new database system. I had volunteered myself for the job not really knowing what it entailed. I wanted to show willing and drifted into it without too much consideration.

Without any warning, I received an appalling appraisal, which put me on a programme of special measures meaning that if I did not meet those targets, I would be out of a job.

I was given six weeks to meet some poorly and loosely set objectives. I was clearly in the wrong job, not working out of my gifts, and I felt it was grossly unfair. I had been cheated and left alone with no support from HR who were toeing the corporate line.

Whilst I tried my hardest to comply with these targets I began to spiral downwards emotionally. I found I had to remove myself from certain situations at work, as I would occasionally break down and cry. I began to drink. Moods swung fast and I started taking antidepressants.

HR suggested I took six weeks off. I attended a day clinic, which specialised in anxiety and depression. I learnt several things while I was there:

- *The usefulness of cognitive behavioural therapy (CBT) and counselling in general. I even considered this as a future career at one point.*
- *My tendency to 'catastrophise' about certain situations.*
- *The reasons why people get into depressive states.*
- *The tools and techniques for relaxation.*
- *The usefulness of group therapy and hearing others stories which were often worse than my own.*

Towards the end of my time off I went on holiday to relax and came back to work feeling better about myself. However the job was still the same, the wrong one, and I failed the test of passing one of the short term objectives set for me. I was sent to Harley Street to see if I was fit to work. Of course I was, it was just I was not working in the right role or environment and it was no longer sustainable.

HR lined me up with some executive coaching with an underlying brief to find a different career path, whether inside or outside the company. That is when I met Lorraine and we began to explore my strengths, skills and personality type as well as gain support for managing my current role. I realised that I am a very strategic person who can easily see the big picture. I am very creative, interested in people and prefer a more flexible approach to work, working at my best when things are unpredictable or in a crisis. These gifts were not appreciated in my current role. When I failed the third and final objective at work, we reached an agreement for me to leave.

I was unemployed for eight months and I became very self-disciplined about honing my CV to new job opportunities. I became quite skilled at presenting what I offered to different jobs where I would add value. I took on short-term contracts, which enriched my CV as it showed different skills I had to offer.

Now I am in a permanent job which is 18 minutes walk from home, compared to a one-hour-plus commute by train. I am still within the same work sector in marketing, although I am being valued for the skills I bring, particularly my tactical strategic direction. The team I work with is highly collaborative compared to the old dictatorial regime of before.

Without considering the impact of my current boss, I would rate the job a 7.5/10 as an overall fit to my SHIFT profile. My current boss is possibly the direct opposite personality type to me – very picky with detail, not great with people and appears to me to be a bit of a bully and insecure about his own abilities, so has a tendency to pull other people down. With the boss in mind I would rate the job a 3 or 4/10, although I hope that he will be moved on soon. If he doesn't, I will. I certainly have come to realise there is nothing I can do to change him for the better.

Throughout this whole experience I have learned to believe in myself so much more, now that I have discovered what really energises me and clarified my skills and preferences. I have also learned perseverance, never to give up, and I am no longer afraid of being made redundant as I know I have marketable skills.

Lessons from Sajid's story

Here are some reflections from Sajid's story to apply to your own career journey:

- Working in the wrong job can have a significant health impact.
- Attending a specialist clinic for depression and anxiety can be extremely useful giving you tools for life.
- Seek help and support if you are in a difficult job to help you discern the next steps. Confidence can be at an all-time low making this difficult to do on your own.
- Taking on interim contract jobs can be a means for earning income, and honing more skills whilst you find the permanent job.
- Your boss can make or break a job even if the job is a good fit for you .
- Persevere, when you are clear about who you are and what you have to offer, it will shine through in interview and you will get there, even if it takes time.

Story 2: Rajula

I was a 'high performer' for two years running and yet I was not getting recognised for the work I was doing. If anything, resources were being taken away from me, I was given little support and I was beginning to think, 'What is wrong with me?' More work was being piled on me. I was being ignored, and when the head of my team was leaving, I had the sense that I was being stopped from applying for the position. It was not a pleasant work environment, even though I knew I was good at my job and was getting good appraisals.

I began to get very stressed, working late to meet the work demands. I reacted late one evening to a colleague's unhelpful remarks, only to find disciplinary action was to be taken against me for my behaviour the following Monday.

That is when HR assigned me to Lorraine for support. We explored the dynamics of what was going on at work, my feelings in relation to it as well as working through my SHIFT model.

In spite of the first few sessions, my mental health began to deteriorate. Sleep was very erratic; I was extremely tired and could not function well. I was very angry about what was going on at work and this was preoccupying me. I finally decided to check in to a psychiatric hospital as it all became too unmanageable. What I learnt there was:

- *The need to take time to reflect and become aware of the 'red flags' of stress.*
- *How therapy groups of different people from all walks of life can help.*
- *The importance of one-to-one therapy.*
- *Relaxation techniques.*
- *Meditation.*

I explored options of returning to my home country, as my visa was a work-related. However work with Lorraine helped me realise that I really wanted to stay in the UK, and other professional advice suggested that even though it was not ideal, going back to my old work place while I recovered would put me in a better place to get another job.

I did go back to work and eventually we came to an agreement for me to leave. I set up as a freelancer which is much more suited to my personality preference. Working through my SHIFT profile earlier confirmed that I was incredibly creative, intuitive, able to see the big picture, so strategy was my strength. I was also a team player and loved working in a team environment, and that I was good in a crisis, preferring flexibility and not too much confining structure.

As a freelance consultant, I was free of the corporate structure and could create a virtual team of associates to whom I could pass work when I had too much to do. I could also bring the whole of my skills and personality to a job without restrictions. Of course there is the unstable prospect of feast or famine financially, which all freelancers face, but currently it is not an issue as I have a steady stream of work.

I still have much to learn about selling myself for the right price although I know this role is a far better fit to who I am. Watch this space as to what I can do now.

Lessons from Rajula's story

Here are some reflections from Rajula's to apply to your own career journey:

- If things are not adding up at work, seek help to explore the underlying dynamics to give you a deeper understanding.

- Where possible, seek help to talk through your feelings about what is going on at work. Forgiving and letting go can be the hardest things to do when the hurt is deep. In my experience, even if you do not forget, forgiveness is one of the keys to moving on and letting go of the horrible past so that a new beginning can emerge (see Managing Transitions model earlier).

- Do not be afraid to use all the psychiatric support you can get. You are being wise to do so. There is no shame in it.

- Unfortunately employers still understand mental health poorly. Be careful how and to whom you disclose any history of mental health issues. Ensure confidentiality boundaries are in place, as much as is possible.

- Working in the wrong environment, even if the job is right, can affect your mental state significantly.

- Going back to the same workplace after taking time out can help you regain health and strength sufficiently to look for another job. It also looks better from a new employer point of view if you are applying from an employed position, unless of course you are going the freelancer route.

- Becoming a freelancer has the benefits of freedom and choosing when and whom you work for. If you are a team player, make sure you network to set up a virtual team of associates (however loosely connected) to bounce ideas off and share some of the workload if necessary.

- Know that when you work from your SHIFT profile in the right environment, anything is possible. I have seen it too many times to not believe it.

Facing the challenge

If you have experienced physical or mental illness in your career, it is a challenging time for you and those around you. The loss of health and how life used to be, however temporary the illness or injury, can be huge. The grieving process for this loss can be short or long-lived. Simply recognising that you might be going through a process of grieving is key to getting started on the road to recovery. As with all challenges, finding appropriate support to help you get through the challenge is crucial for your long-term wellbeing. (See the Support and Challenge Model in Chapter 8).

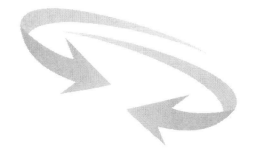

Chapter 7
ADVERSITY

Adversity shapes us, and can shape us in ways that create a passion within us to ensure others don't have to suffer in the same way. Just like when a fire burns back the bushes and undergrowth. Out of the ashes, new growth emerges. Here are three people who have experienced emotional or physical pain in different circumstances and who have used their pain to shape their careers.

Story 1: Peter

I first met Lorraine in 2000 when we were working for the same coaching and training company. She was an executive coach and I was attending the coaching training as well as implementing IT systems for the company. Before joining this company, I had worked in Software Development for eighteen years. During that time I had set up a department, recruited the right staff and run a team developing new and emerging computer systems. However, the one problem with this job was my boss. I thought I could change him, but I couldn't. Eventually we fell out over a project and the Sales Director and I handed in our notice on the same day. I had no other work to go to, and a family with three young daughters to support, but I knew I could no longer work there. I left with a huge sense of relief.

Meanwhile, my wife and I were trying to work out how to best educate and support our three daughters who were all diagnosed with dyslexia.

After her school told us they could do nothing for our eldest we managed to find a nurturing private school to support all three children through their primary years. Always willing to be involved, my wife set up a parent-teacher group before becoming chair of governors, and I offered my support in various ways to help with the running of the school.

Eventually we ran into our next challenge: secondary education. The schools near us were either far too academic or not a place you would send a quiet, dyslexic, well-behaved girl. After running out of ideas we decided to look into setting up our own school. We figured that if we had difficulties in this area, there would be other parents in similar situations. Alongside my experience of business and my wife's as chair of governors we found three very keen educationalists who shared our passion to help a child grow according to their gifts.

After much planning and advertising we rented a hall in an accessible part of London, advertised the school and started our first year with twelve children. At that stage the school was run by our friend James, with my wife supporting him. I was still working full-time for the coaching and training company, as the school could not afford the income I needed to support my family.

It was at this point that Lorraine suggested that we work together on my SHIFT profile, to help me focus my career direction and explore some of the barriers to action. She asked me lots of challenging questions, which helped me to articulate what I already knew in my heart but was avoiding. With her encouragement I was able to face up to these issues and take action.

One insight gained was that I have always set things up from scratch, got things going, and have a passion for problem solving. My heart was, of course, in the set-up of the school – this was my children's future at stake. Another driving force for my involvement in the school was that I realised that I too am dyslexic. For most of my schooling I was always at the bottom of the class, thought I was an idiot, and had lost all confidence by the time I left school with a few O Levels. It was only on a BTEC course – where I could specialise in the areas of my gifting – that I succeeded. I later went on to complete a PhD in computing.

However whilst my heart was clear – I wanted to help run the school full-time – there were still too many barriers in the way. The embryonic school was unable to support my wage and I knew little about teaching or teenagers. It would have been so easy to say 'I don't have the skills, so I can't do this.'

Exploring these barriers with Lorraine helped me to dive in at the deep end and take a risk. It felt like a 'calling'. We were fortunate that we had a low mortgage and an inexpensive lifestyle, but looking back now I don't know how we did it. We believed in the school and what we could achieve and that was the most important thing.

A year after the school was set up, I went full-time. Whilst I am now the head of the school, my IT skills are always put to good use to provide the best and simplest systems, which enable our pupils to thrive. No skill you learn along the way is ever wasted.

From twelve pupils in a school hall, we now own a whole building and have a roll of 125. Pupils are valued as unique individuals and the school works to find the gifts and talents in each one, with the belief that the development of character and integrity are more important than academics. Pupils come from a wide spectrum and we deliberately include some with special education needs such as Asperger's Syndrome or dyslexia. We are looking forward to moving to a new site and expand our curriculum into A Levels.

I believe there are two reasons for our success, even though it has been a rollercoaster ride at times. We believed in the idea of the school but our confidence was low, so initially we had to step out and believe we had the skills to do it, to convince others to join us on the journey. We learned from every situation and adapted accordingly until we grew more skills and confidence. Secondly, we believe that our uniqueness lies in our relationships with our parents. Many schools do not communicate well with parents, but we think of them as customers and treat them accordingly.

The biggest lesson I've learned from this journey is to step up into leadership even if you are a reluctant leader. When you believe in what you are doing with all your heart, the rest (skills and knowledge) can follow. You just need to trust there will be a way forward.

Lessons from Peter's story

Here are some reflections from Peter's story to apply to your own career journey:

- Even if you are in the right job a 'bad boss' can ruin it. It is unlikely you will be able to change them, so you may need to take action.

- Even if it seems illogical, sometimes it might be necessary to leave a job without anything to go to, as long as you weigh up the risks and benefits first.

- If, like Peter, you have felt you were at the bottom of the class and an 'idiot' at school, it probably means that you were not operating out of your gifting (or SHIFT profile). When you do, you are much more likely to be fruitful. I know this to be the case from the many people with whom I have worked.

- 'Know the risks, and do it anyway'. You may not have all the skills yet but you know your heart and you just need to find ways of building those skills and finding the right support (See the Support and Challenge model in Chapter 8).

- Explore the barriers to following your heart and articulate them, then find ways to reduce the barriers, making it safe enough for you to leap.

- Make sure you have a unique offering in what you do, to make you stand out from the crowd – just be YOU – the more you become who you really are, the more satisfied and successful you will be in your work.

- No skills that you learn on your career journey are ever wasted.

Story 2: Ling

I always thought I wanted to become a doctor but when I flunked my A levels, my dreams were shattered and I ended up doing a Physics degree since I managed to secure a place through clearing. Physics at degree level was very different from school and I limped miserably along the course, finishing up with a third. Determined to never be involved in the world of Physics again, I applied for graduate training schemes at 2 well known clothing retailers as well as a job working for the British Council in Japan.

I arrived 45 minutes late to an assessment day at my first choice graduate training scheme. The other candidates were already in the middle of working out a business case study. I thought I had blown my chances from the outset for being so spectacularly late and was completely surprised when they offered me the job at the end of the assessment. I was offered a position on the basis that I just got on with the work, got stuck in and kept my calm, showing the assessors that I would be capable of handling stressful situations well.

I was also offered a job with the other clothing retailer but deferred both positions for a year to take up the teaching post in Japan. The programme was extremely tough as little support or training was provided before I was literally left in a small remote Japanese village on my own and expected to teach English at the local primary school. Quite stressful. For some, this programme was too isolating, though I took every opportunity I could to make the best of it, learning Japanese as a matter of survival and then learning how to ski as that was the only thing to do locally. Through that year, I learned that it is OK not to know the answer to everything, that I have the ability to find out the information I need, that I have initiative and could use it – a life lesson that has stood me in good stead.

When I returned to England, I joined the clothing retailer as a graduate trainee working on the shop floor, learning how to manage a small department. I learned management skills as well as the basics of how to run a small profitable department. With Sunday trading being introduced, I transferred to a high street retailer as a merchandiser in their head office. Here, I learned how to run a business. The buyer would decide on trends to follow and decide what type of colours and fabrics were in fashion and I would work out a business case for it, what price to sell at, how much stock to purchase and so on. I was working at my best, using my skills and it was an 8 or 9/10 job.

By this stage, I'd got married, and a few years later had my first child. I had always seen my calling to be a mother and had lofty ideas that I would be the ultimate 'Earth mother', always being there for my children and not working. I had a very difficult birth and nearly died so my introduction to early motherhood was tricky. On top of that, I had a baby who did not seem to do what I wanted it to do – not surprisingly, it was a big learning adjustment.

I started to work for an ex-colleague as a freelance trainer two or three days a week, which gave me more flexibility than working in London. It was exciting and a good money earner but not really what I wanted to do. I decided to train as a pregnancy yoga teacher because I had the desire to help other young mums avoid the traumatic birth process I had endured and I could also work around my family's needs. In addition, there was no one else doing this work where I lived so I went about training and setting up my own business alongside the freelance work. It seemed like a no brainer.

All that business management I had learned in retailing came in very useful as I set up my pregnancy yoga business. I started with one class a week, which quickly grew to five classes a week, all within school hours. I was helping other women learn what it meant to become a mother through getting in touch emotionally and physically with themselves and their unborn child. I had found my 10/10 job!

After my second child, my pregnancy yoga business had grown so much that I stopped my freelancing work. I was doing a job I had passion about, born out of my own pain. And it was hugely successful. After my third child, it was obvious I had to stop work as juggling work with the needs of three children was exhausting. What's more, I had a son with dyslexia and dyspraxia and there was a great need to be at home to support him. I handed my pregnancy yoga business over to a trusted friend and discovered I was now mentally in the place to be the 'Earth mother' I thought I would be in the early years.

I know some day I could re-start my business again if I wanted to, although for the next season it is about supporting my family, as I know they will only be with me a short time before they spread their wings and leave home. I realise I am very fortunate to be able to do this financially, although I know I will want to work again when the time is right, for my own sake. Watch this space!

Lessons from Ling's story

Here are some reflections from Ling's story to apply to your own career journey:

- Doing a degree by default may not be the best solution as it means three years of doing something you are not passionate about. However for some it still might be the best option as long as you can at least get a third. Your exam results for some jobs are not so relevant as long as you have a degree.

- Once you get to an assessment, showing your initiative and being you, can be what it takes to get the job, even if you turn up 45 minutes late (although I wouldn't recommend being late).

- Gap years can stretch you in ways you would not imagine, giving you opportunities to use your initiative and, in this case, realise that it is 'OK not to know everything' because there is always someone to ask who might know – an important life lesson.

- Painful or difficult situations can be a catalyst for a passion to improve things for others from which a new business emerges.

- Nothing is ever wasted. Skills you learn in an earlier role can support you later in new roles, unexpectedly.

- It is OK to 'just be a mum or just be a dad' and not work. I hear this phrase so often, which in our culture seems to devalue these extremely important roles. For some this is not financially possible so there is a need for part- or full-time work. Others may need to strike a balance between home duties and mental stimulation, regardless of the finances, as they know they will make better spouses and parents as a result. It is different for every family and there is no right and wrong way to bring up our children – just your way that brings you most happiness as a family.

- As our children get older, a new season of opportunity emerges where we have more scope to explore new challenges. They are not with us for long so make the most of now.

Story 3: Martha

I really lacked confidence after I left school, so I took two years out. I was thirsty for adventure so went on my first expedition to Indonesia where I felt fully alive in the jungle. I also spent time in Japan teaching English to businessmen. Could I survive the urban jungle? For £80 an hour it was worth it.

I finally ended up working with horses, one of my hobbies, as I loved the freedom of riding through open green space. Although it was a hard graft, I thoroughly loved learning to be an instructor. Eventually I decided my brain needed more than this and so I applied to Edinburgh University to study archaeology and social anthropology.

At university I became a successful rower and was on the long list for the Commonwealth Games along with rowing champion, Cath Grainger. I had to make a decision, spend time rowing or get a degree. I finished my degree and was also an officer in the TA and was fast-tracked to Sandhurst. I was fuelled by insecurity to challenge myself and overcome my lack of confidence. Although deep down I had a belief that anything was possible. I had a choice of going on a safe John Lewis Graduate Scheme or working as a supervisor for the Mighty Cleaning Company.

I went the 'road less travelled' and cleaned loos for a month in an airport before taking up my supervisory role. However I was more interested in the cleaners as people rather than the role or the company. Having left to take on a business development role, I was made redundant six months later so applied to World Challenge to lead expeditions to Mexico. I was living in the slums of Mexico, experiencing the pure joy of people there who had so little in material terms.

I finally returned to the UK and started work at Goldman Sachs as a project manager, later transferring into HR to manage the coaches and trainers used by the company. However what I really wanted to do was to coach and train myself. I later joined a coaching and training organisation, Mast, where I trained presentation skills amongst other things.

I still work for Mast very part-time, mostly for my own sanity. I now have four children. As a mother, my self-worth plummeted and working gave me more energy for the kids, not less. After my third child I found it very difficult to cope with three children under three screaming at me and I experienced quite bad postnatal depression.

Through this very low time, I suddenly found myself wondering how many other mums were experiencing the same as I was and who were living perhaps in the same road or nearby? How could we support each other? The idea of Mums 4 Mums emerged: a network of mums, who are there for other mums in the community. Groups started up, including an art group, cricket club, choir and a cooking club. After six months, one member of the community said 'I have lived in Acton for six months being a doctor, I now cannot go down the street without knowing anyone.'

The Acton Mums 4 Mums still continues, using Yahoo to connect online. After moving to Amersham, I set up the Amersham branch, where members of the community regularly meet for coffee and attend workshops on small business development and parenting amongst others. Often at these networking meetings, mums looking for a lawyer, or a coach to support their small business would meet someone who could offer just that – all in the comfort of my home around the kitchen table. At one meeting a member said 'I have lived opposite Zara for five to ten years and we have now only just met.'

Whilst Mums 4 Mums is a charity rather than a money making enterprise, it has been born out of the pain of feeling alone, isolated and overwhelmed with the responsibility of raising four children. The common theme through all the roles I have done is leadership; whether in the army as a troop commander, leading expeditions or coaching and training. I love starting new things and have an innate ability for new ideas. My main purpose and 'heart' in life, which I cannot stop myself doing wherever I am, is to inspire others to get unstuck and move on, improving their sense of self-worth.

I have had a desire for adventure all my life and I have gone with the flow when looking back at my career. It is OK not to have a plan, although I have found the key is to keep noticing what energises you at each step and move closer towards it. Before I could not value myself as I am. I was only as valuable as the last adventure or achievement. I was searching for paternal approval. I had to let go of my dreams of a career.

I have now come to accept that just being there for the children and being vulnerable is OK. I am good enough, although obviously not perfect, and I will no doubt always find an outlet to support others on top of my duties as a wife and parent.

Lessons from Martha's story

Here are some reflections from Martha's story to apply to your own career journey:

- Insecurity and a lack of confidence can be the fuel to achieve and feel a sense of self-worth. Begin to raise your awareness about what is causing this through support from counsellors or through prayer ministry, if you find that helpful.

- Going with the flow without a plan is fine. Just make sure you move to more energising roles each time you step forward. Try and avoid the drift approach and being stuck in a role for too long where you feel trapped by your circumstances – there is always an alternative if you want to accept the implications.

- If you are experiencing adversity, think how can this experience be put to the good of other people?

- Learning to value yourself just as you are can take a lifetime. You are 'good enough' just as you are. Do you believe this?

Chapter 8
FAMILY

In this chapter I have described my own journey and those of others managing careers while having children. Every family is different and each family has a different financial set-up that requires parents to keep earning to pay the bills. There is no right or wrong way of managing your career when you have a family. My only encouragement would be to keep focused on the long-term vision and make incremental steps towards it, however small.

My story

Before I had my first son, Sam, I was working four days a week and focusing one day a week on my Gestalt masters degree. I was working in a role that fitted my SHIFT profile and loving it. Thanks to low cost accommodation at the time and some savings, I had the fortune of not being forced back to work for financial reasons after our son's birth.

I adored our new son and could not have wished for an easier first baby to learn the ropes of motherhood. Sam was a complete delight and got named the smiliest boy in Northwood. For all his smiles though, the biggest thing I struggled with, other than endless nappies and sleepless nights, was my identity.

Who was I when I was no longer working? Where was my worth when I was no longer earning? My childhood experience was of a mother who was ill, who did not work and was fairly helpless. My biggest fear was becoming like her, dependent on her husband and financially helpless.

When Sam was one, I decided to complete my second year towards my masters in Gestalt psychology. This was helping me edge that bit closer to being more proficient in my job as well as giving me a mental focus. I was still looking after Sam full-time, although Rob looked after him when I went to college one evening a week. I soon learnt that Sam's nap times were essay-writing times, and I was very thankful to have a husband who is great with babies.

Whilst my identity had been wrapped up in my work, I loved it, it was part of who I am. It was a real challenge to realise my calling as a wife and mother is far higher than my call to work. In fact, I believe the biggest and most privileged job in the whole world is becoming a parent, and it is the hardest with the least training. It is a huge honour to be given children to look after as not all couples get that opportunity, and yet it is the most life-changing and challenging role I certainly have ever experienced. I found it was far easier to work than playing mind-numbing imaginary games, however important that was.

When Sam was two-and-a-half, by some coincidence I was introduced to a new executive coaching group. Its members were keen for me to join them on a very part-time basis (four days a month). As Rob was working full-time, I recruited support for occasional trips into London. When I first started back with a new coaching client I remember very vividly how my confidence was completely shot. What did I know about coaching? Would clients really pay me after my brain had gone to mush these last few years? Could I remember all the models and tools that I had learned? Would I let the new executive coaching company down in some way? Endless doubt!

At the end of my first coaching session, the client ended up in tears and had decided I was the right match to support her in her own development. I came away from that session thinking 'I obviously made a connection but I didn't do much, just listen, and they want to pay me.' It took a while for the confidence to come back, although the more I did the more confidence returned.

After about a year, we moved to our own house and had our second son Josh when Sam was three-and-a-half. Having worked through the identity issue, this was now not my main challenge. I adored Josh as much as I did Sam.

Josh was a delightful baby and like his personality, he was extremely active, particularly at night. He got to five months and through the sleeplessness, I began to lose the plot, mentally. I was so exhausted I sought help from a psychiatrist who thankfully told me it was normal and I just needed sleep – phew – I wasn't going mad – but it had got that bad. Bless him, Josh still remains very active and always puts a smile on my face. That so makes up for the sleepless nights.

As far as work was concerned, although we had bought our first house, I was again fortunate enough not to have to go back to work for financial reasons. Slightly earlier than I had planned, I was invited back to take on a client or two just before Josh was a year old. Again this was extremely part-time and I managed to get local flexible support for childcare (four short days a month I think was my max), where I would dash into London, do a session and come home again, but the energy work gave me meant I was fresher for the children and had more energy to give them on my return.

Whilst I was coaching one-to-one, I missed doing facilitation with teams and groups, which I had avoided as it would have been too long away from the boys. So when the local church wanted to run a course called Growing Leaders[xv], I jumped at it as I could do this in the evening, once a month and train leaders in some of the models I used with clients as well as connect it to leadership models in the Bible. It got me back in the saddle of facilitation, which by that stage I had not done for four years, and it grew my confidence in it once again.

I continued to work very part-time as an executive coach until the boys were at school or nursery. I would dash into London during school times and dash back to pick them up. Oh the energy I had – it could only have come from the fact that when I work I have more energy than before I start. In my experience this is what happens when you work from your SHIFT profile. The bombshell then came when Rob was made redundant after 15 years working for his college and three months later, I was diagnosed with cancer. The boys were 8 and 5. Josh had just started school. I had just increased my workload a little as we knew Rob's job was looking dubious.

Once I had recovered sufficiently from the cancer treatment, I slowly re-introduced myself to my work clients. Rob got his photography business up and running. We were now both self-employed which meant we were living the 'feast and famine' experience of so many self-employed people. With it though came the possibility to share the childcare. Whoever won the contracts, the other would look after the children. We did have back-up support occasionally but in the most part, we were fortunate enough to share the childcare between us.

This pattern has continued until of course the brain tumour hit in 2014. After then it was a journey of recovery, adjustment and regaining enough energy to address my primary calling as a wife and mother. Just regaining sufficient energy to function at home and support Rob and the boys in hopefully a better way has been a big part of the recovery process.

I have to say that because I get so much energy from my work, just two months after coming out of the hospice, still fragile, not walking well, with shot balance, I undertook some SHIFT work with one private client, passed on by a friend, on the understanding that if I was not up to it that day, I could cancel. I completed the work with my client and realised that even in my very limited physical condition I could still be effective in encouraging others to step further into their SHIFT profile, from my armchair this time. I had SHIFTED my career once again.

Lessons from my story

Here are some reflections from my story to apply to your own career journey:

- However tough it is, know that your calling as a spouse and a parent comes before your career. This has taken me a long time to learn, as work for me gave me so much energy. I have often got the order the wrong way round.
- Stopping work for any length of time can cause you to challenge your identity. Our identity ultimately lies in who we are not what we do.
- Not everyone has sufficient funds or a flexible spouse able to help with the childcare. In the end as parents, we all do the best we can with the resources and circumstances we have.
- If you are working from your SHIFT profile you will be getting more energy out of working than not. If this is the case sometimes it is beneficial to do a little work, as opposed to none, as the family will benefit from your renewed energy.
- If your physical limitations initially restrict you, you will find a way to SHIFT again in a different setting perhaps, however unlikely that seems.

Story 1: Ricardo

I was working in a communications department for a university. I am a journalist by profession. I was commuting up to 20 hours a week and when our first son came along, I knew I had to find a more local and flexible job as my wife also needed to work full-time as a journalist in London. The childcare drop-offs and pick-ups needed to be managed between us.

I therefore joined a communications consultancy with a 30-minute commute. At the interview, I thought I had been clear about my responsibilities as a parent and how working late and out of hours was not a possibility. I also had a sense at interview stage that the role would be relatively senior and strategic, playing to my personality strengths.

The reality was that I was expected to work late and occasionally at weekends, my personal values did not match the organisation's and the job was not as strategic as they said it would be. There was a mismatch in spite of the commute time being better. After four months, we came to an agreement that the job was not working out for either of us. I went on holiday and came back offering to work out my notice while I considered other jobs. They insisted I took gardening leave and I went straight away. This was a real shock, although the right decision in hindsight. It was, though, a huge blow to my confidence.

Now that I was redundant, I suddenly had more time to look after my son and it was very liberating to spend quality time with him, going to playgrounds and soft play areas. I was one of the few lucky dads amongst all those mums, being there for my child. It was very relaxed. During this time I decided to look for support for my career and that is when I contacted Lorraine. Articulating my story and exploring the SHIFT model helped me see the next steps to take.

I knew I had to get another job as the bills were mounting and the mortgage needed paying. I felt quite scared I could lose the house or not get another job at the same level. One thing I knew was I didn't want to make the mistake I made last time and wanted to have more certainty that the next role would match my family life in a better way. Unexpectedly, during the exploration of my SHIFT model, we discussed the fact that I often experienced panic attacks. I was encouraged to seek counselling, which I did, and discovered specific medication that has completely transformed my life. After 17 years I am now anxiety-free and a better husband and father as a result.

I applied for a job, and I had a panic attack at the interview. It definitely felt wrong and my body was giving me clear indicators not to pursue it. Finally I applied to a charity, which supported vulnerable young children. My role is as an internal communications officer. I used my SHIFT notes as a checklist and had a really good sense that this next role was a better match of my Top 10 skills and the commute time was now 20 minutes. What's more, even though the position was not as senior as I would have liked, I had no panic attacks at the interview. I performed well on the day and it just felt right.

The previous job I was in, I would have rated 3/10 when comparing it to my SHIFT profile. This new job is a 7 or 8. To reach my ideal SHIFTed career from here I would have to go to four days a week, have a more senior role or better still, become self-employed and set up a business with my journalist wife, supporting charities with copy writing and sharing the childcare duties between us. This last idea though feels a little daunting with the uncertainty of bills being paid, although would definitely score a 10 if I could make it happen at some point in the future.

Lessons from Ricardo's story

Here are some reflections from Ricardo's story to apply to your own career journey:

- Work out your ideal commute time and apply for roles within that distance from home.

- Be really clear at interview what your work boundaries and expectations are and where you can and cannot compromise.

- Once you have worked out your SHIFT profile, don't be swayed by one aspect of your working environment (e.g. commute) to take the job – it could be a wrong move.

- Exploring SHIFT can give you more time for reflection on other aspects of your life e.g. mental health. Getting the right help might be life changing.

- Being made redundant can sometimes be a gift. Now that you are not working, what more can you do that you couldn't before?

- Redundancy can hugely knock your confidence so get the support you can from wherever you can.

- Listen to your body (such as Ricardo's panic attacks). What is it saying to you?
- Aspire to the best working set up for your family and see if you can make it happen. Children are only with you a short time before they fly the nest.

Story 2: Jacqueline

I was a business studies graduate who could speak good German, as my mother is German. To improve my language skills I worked for a couple of companies in Germany for five years, where I met my English husband.

We moved back to England where I worked in the marketing department for a well-known financial institution. My boss was the best boss I have ever had, nurturing yet challenging. He believed in me and told me he did not want to see me in the same job after two years or something was wrong. His whole ambition was to coach me, to know everything that he knew and more. It was very freeing.

I followed my husband back to Germany working for a different department in the same company. I had my first child there and had the financial support to not need to go back to work. Although I wasn't working I took up several voluntary positions including setting up a mums and toddlers group and other support groups for young mothers, which of course helped me with the newness of motherhood. We moved back to England again. After my second child was born I was getting the itch to go back to work. I met someone on holiday who told me all about counselling and it sounded fascinating.

When my third child was one I took my psychology A level. Later I embarked on a part-time diploma in counselling, although I had no idea if I was going to be paid and be employed as one in the end. I just loved the self-exploration. For a counselling placement I began working for a school as a student counsellor and formed a good relationship with the head, who later employed me within school hours. I was adding value and they appreciated the work I was doing. I later trained as a family therapist and did this for about a year and a half, although it did not fit well with the family needs so I gave up. It was very demanding and not very supportive and therefore quite stressful.

I had a family room added on as an extension, which I have used for private clients. I love training, lecturing and facilitation and have been using these skills in a variety of different ways, lecturing at a local college, running 'retreat' days for women, running workshops for young children transitioning to secondary school, to name a few.

After working through the SHIFT model and personality profile, it confirmed to me my Top 10 skills that I loved using and highlighted my need to be part of a team where there could be a bit of flexibility and structure at the same time. I would love to work in a centre or in a team where my counselling and teaching was used on the side, in a supportive environment. I also have a passion to change cultures for the better.

The head of pastoral care at the school where I work recently told me she was leaving and that her post was being advertised. Immediately, without thinking, I said I would jump at the chance of working in a team in a supportive environment doing what I love doing. I'm not sure if it will go anywhere but I am certainly getting clearer about where I step next.

Lessons from Jacqueline's story

Here are some reflections from Jacquleine's story to apply to your own career journey:

- Find a boss who believes in you and you will be amazed how much you can do.
- Learn something new that really interests you irrespective of whether it will turn into financial gain – there are plenty of free courses or cheap courses online or bursaries available if finances are an issue.
- Use your networks to get your next job – it is largely who you know that gets you the job rather than applying coldly.
- Try out different ways of working using your top skills. If it is too stressful, notice this and adjust accordingly – it won't be sustainable over time. The role has to energise you to be sustainable ideally or perhaps it is a variety of roles that will energise you?
- Create your own work environment in your home to give you more options about where you work.
- Think big even if it seems impossible – what role would you ideally want and in what environment – what do you dream of?
- SHIFT can help you get really clear about the next step in your career.

Support and challenge model

One of the first models that Victoria Cassells taught me was fairly simple but very effective. Jacqueline's story reminds me of this.

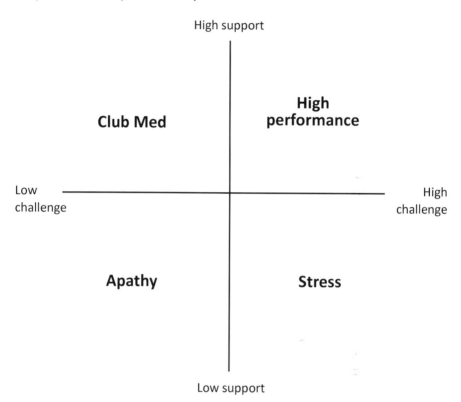

As with all challenges, finding appropriate support to help you get through the challenge is crucial for your long-term well-being. For example, whilst Jacqueline enjoyed being a family therapist and was good at it, the challenge was high and the support was low. She ended up feeling quite stressed. It was not surprising that after a year or so she decided to stop family therapy. When anyone operates in the Stress Box for too long, it can lead to burnout. Being in the Stress Box for a while though can be stimulating and rewarding, for example resolving a crisis. However, the aim is always to move yourself into the high performance box eventually.

To continue as a high-performing family therapist, Jacqueline would need to put more support in place to meet the challenge. For example, could her husband be home one night a week? Could she identify a supportive team to work with? Could her supervisor support her more effectively? Could there be greater peer support from fellow family counsellors? Putting these things in place would move Jacqueline from the Stress Box to High-performing Box.

When anyone operates in the Stress Box for too long, there is sometimes a need to move to the Club Med Box to recover. Here there is plenty of support and very little challenge. A chance to recharge and feel nurtured before feeling ready to take on any more challenges. The Club Med Box is fine for a while and very relaxing. It could be represented by an actual physical holiday or a job where the boss is great at nurturing you and giving you all the support you need although does not challenge you too much. Eventually boredom and frustration will set in and you will need to increase the challenge by changing roles or going back to work, to once again move into high performance.

Nick had taken a career break for over two years (Club Med). He was a very successful IT executive who was becoming increasingly unhappy and stressed by his work. Boldly he decided to take a career break and focus on his family. He was fortunate though to have sufficient savings to do this. He is now ready to re-engage with work and really find a role where the challenge is something he is passionate about and the support is much higher than in his previous role.

The remaining box, Apathy, is where the support is low and the challenge is low, which can lead to sense of 'why bother as there is no challenge to meet and nobody appears to care'. People do not stay long in this box usually unless they are stuck by external circumstances.

One e-commerce executive I worked with was in apathy for a while. Every time I met him, he gazed down at the floor. He was hunched up with extremely low energy. He had got to the top of his department and could do the job standing on his head. He didn't need much support for his job, but did need a lot of support to help him move from apathy to high performance. He was in a large corporation, being paid very well, which meant he felt trapped. The salary paid for school fees and the standard of living he and his family had become accustomed to. Yet he was hugely de-motivated and unhappy.

Thankfully, with a bit of support, my client managed to realise that he was born to be an entrepreneur, and for the sake of his health and for his family, he finally left work to set up his own business. When I contacted him about a year later, he told me he was the luckiest person alive. Not only was he earning more than he did before, he was now loving what he was doing and could take as many holidays as he wanted. Result!

Which box are you mostly operating from in your current role? What do you need to do to increase or decrease the support and challenge so that you are operating from the High-performance Box?

Chapter 9
NO JOB

This chapter is for those who may be:

- Made redundant.

- Trained in a particular profession and found there are no opportunities for recruitment.

- Retiring.

I have been fortunate not to be made redundant, although I have experienced this second hand when my husband was made redundant. I have though had at least two jobs where I was treading water, trying to find a way out and feeling very frustrated that new jobs were not opening up. It was tedious and I felt very stuck. I had good advice from a mentor though, which in essence said 'stick to the knitting until something better emerges'.

Some people though do not get the option to stick to the knitting, as we have seen with Ricardo in chapter 7. The same was the case with Steven in my next case study. Once the job has gone for whatever reason, how do you keep going emotionally, financially, physically and spiritually? Everyone is different and every work situation is different. I hope these case studies give you some food for thought to help you explore how you will 'mind the gap' between jobs, if this is your situation.

Story 1: Steven, made redundant after 20 years

I was working in the marketing department of a large company, a middle manager position with a team of five managers. There was a cultural shift in the organisation to raise performance standards. On the surface this seemed like a good idea but there were many in the company, including myself, who felt that the programme was being used as a means of 'exiting' people from the business through performance ratings. Although I had a good track record at appraisals, I began to collect evidence of my performance to track my progress ready for the next appraisal. At that appraisal I was told that I was not meeting the required standard.

After more than 19 years during which my work was commended, it was now found wanting without adequate specific feedback as to the reasons why. I became quite angry about what was happening to me and to my colleagues. I thought long and hard about whether to go to tribunal to raise my concerns. A good friend advised me not to go down that route as the stress would be significant and too high a price to pay.

In the end we came to an agreement to terminate my employment. I found the process very isolating and painful. Being the main income earner and having had a secure job all these years, it felt quite scary. I managed to get through this stage of being without a job by:

- *Reading the Psalms in the Bible for the whole year.*

- *Going on lots of walks.*

- *Going on two holidays unexpectedly paid for by family.*

- *Conversations with a good friend who was a successful businessman and had experience of redundancy. His particular advice to me was to attend interviews with a vision of what the new job might look like given the information I could glean beforehand and about the industry. This really helped me get my next role.*

- *Spending time with a friend who was a coach and who helped me understand my personality profile.*

- *Playing more sport*

- *Understanding friends who could relate to my situation at a deep level.*

- *Friends offering meals.*

- *Joining recruitment agencies – I had very positive feedback from interviews that helped to build my confidence and helped me understand my marketable skills.*

- *Applying for two jobs a day was my goal and almost a job in itself.*

- *Setting out a contingency plan with my wife depending on how long I was going to be out of work was incredibly useful. We worked out that:*

  - *After six months, if I were not successful, my wife would look for additional work.*

  - *After 9 months I would do contract work.*

  - *After 12 months we would let our house and rent a studio flat.*

  - *After 12-15 months we would need to sell the house and move to a cheaper area.*

When we actually confronted the worst-case scenario and our worst fears, we realised it was not that bad – we would not lose our friends or family, which were far more important: a good thing to realise.

The biggest thing I did to help me work through this painful period was to learn to forgive individuals who had hurt me or let me down, and to let go. This was huge. I felt the need to go through and name them one by one and forgive them out loud for the things they had said and done. I liken it to a having a tape in my head telling me that 'I am rubbish at my job'. I had to re-programme the message to the truth of the earlier years, which told me otherwise.

In spite of all my job applications, which probably amounted to about 80, I got my new job through networking. The post had not been advertised and the job description not fully finalised but because of a contact, I managed to get an interview. The role had two elements – one with which I was familiar and one which was totally new. I bought a book related to the unfamiliar aspects of the job. During the interview I presented information I had gleaned from the book and applied it to the new role.

I met at least six people from the team including the Chief Executive. An organisation's culture almost always stems from the leadership style of the Chief Executive. The culture seemed much more trustworthy than the culture I had come, which I felt was more of a 'blame culture' where people lived in fear of losing their jobs. Whilst my new boss interviewed me, I interviewed him just as much. His hands-off approach appealed and when I joined the company I had a sense that what I did was needed and valued. The size of the organisation also appealed to me – approximately 55 employees compared to thousands. The company was much more personable as a result. What is more, I ended up with better pay than in my old job.

I had only been out of work for three months, although living with the uncertainty of redundancy for nine months. The biggest difference between the two organisations was trust. I would have scored my first company 3/10 on trust and my new company 9/10. I have finally found a better work environment in which my skills are appreciated.

Lessons from Steven's story

Here are some reflections from Steven's story to apply to your own career journey:

- If your job is looking uncertain for any reason, build evidence of your successes to be able to present these before an appraisal or to help maintain your confidence if you are made redundant and are looking for a new job.
- Raising grievances and taking a company to tribunal is an option. However, this can be a very stressful course of action. The physical and emotional cost may not be worth it. There may be an alternative path out of the company that is less costly to you, and from which where you still benefit.
- Think about exercise in different forms to manage the lows of redundancy.
- Surround yourself with good, resourceful friends.
- Go on holiday.
- Set out a contingency plan.
- Structure your day where you can.

- Network, it is far more effective than applying for jobs cold.

- Confront your fears, it may not be that bad in the end and almost a blessing to have time out (see Ricardo, Chapter 8).

- Actively forgive those who have wounded you along the way – this is the biggest step in recovering emotionally.

- You may need to re-programme your mind to remember what is true about your skills and abilities. Help from a listening friend who knows you well or counsellor might be helpful.

- Be proactive in your interviews by imagining how you would carry out the role, given what you know about it. This may make you stand out from the crowd.

- Meet as many of the staff as you can at interviews. You are interviewing them as much as them you. Can you work with the Chief Executive and the culture that he/she generates? What are your criteria for an 'ideal boss'. How does your prospective new boss match up?

- How does the size of the organisation suit you?

- What is the level of trust in the organisation? Ask people at interview or offer to spend a day in the organisation before accepting the job, and ask people you brush shoulders with, if this is possible.

Changing tack

I always liken these uncertain times to a boat sailing through choppy water. The boat is upright, sails fully extended. Although it is being tossed about on the rough sea, it has a rudder. However it is not sure what the destination is and how to chart itself through the wind and waves to get there. The sailor needs to ask the right people to join him or her on the boat, people who have the right skills and ability to help navigate the right course. Who do you need to invite into the boat? What roles do they need to play for you? What can you give back in return? Once the boat is stabilised, a new destination emerges on the horizon and it becomes slowly clearer how the boat needs to tack to get there, depending on the wind direction.

The level of trust within an organisation is key

Steven's story reminds me of a very useful model by Patrick Lencioni which explores *The Five Dysfunctions of a Team*[xvi.] In my version of this model, I like to reverse his terms to suggest there are five functions that make great teams.

The first and foremost of these is trust. How much trust is there in the organisation? How open and honest can you be? Is it OK to make mistakes as long as you own them and improve by them? If trust is low, as with Steven's first job, generally there is a high level of covering your own back, politics, lack of honesty and openness. At its worst the environment can feel toxic. Results in the end will suffer. If the trust is high, as it is with Steven's second job, the environment is much more positive. Experimenting and learning is encouraged. Teamwork is more apparent, there is less micro-management. Conflict is resolved more easily. The team are committed to a common goal. Individuals are accountable to each other and, not surprisingly, results are achieved.

Trust in an organisation, however you define it, is the foundation for any team to be successful. In whatever way you can, find out what levels of trust there are in the organisation you are about to join by asking some of the following questions:

- How 'political' is this organisation on a scale of 1-10?

- How would you rate trust in this organisation on a scale of 1-10? How is this shown?

- What is the style of the Chief Executive? A micro-manager or someone who delegates and lets his/her team deliver? Is there evidence of this from those working with the Chief Executive? There are times when a leader thinks they are delegating, but struggles to fully trust others do the job well for them. The result is they subtly undermine healthy team culture as they micro-manage or critique behind colleagues' backs. For the most part, trust from the Chief Executive will set the culture of the organisation.

The following shows a quick overview of the model, and some of the factors that get in the way of teams being great teams. It starts with trust. Without it, think again as to whether you want to join the organisation as results are unlikely to follow.

As difficult as teamwork can be to achieve, it is not complicated.

The true measure of a team is that it accomplishes the results that it sets out to achieve. To do that on a consistent, ongoing basis a team must develop the five essential functions of a team listed here by embodying the behaviours described for each one.

1: Trust Members of great teams trust one another at a fundamental level, and they are comfortable being vulnerable with each other about their weaknesses, mistakes, fears, and behaviours. They get to a point where they can be completely open with one another, without filters. This is essential to enable teams to...

2: Manage conflict Teams that trust one another are not afraid to engage in robust dialogue around issues and decisions that are key to the organisation's success. They do not hesitate to disagree with, challenge, and question one another, all in the spirit of finding the best answers and making great decisions. This is essential to enable teams to achieve a high level of...

3: Commitment Teams that engage in unfiltered conflict are able to achieve genuine 'buy-in' around important decisions, even when various members of the team initially disagree. That's because they ensure that all opinions and ideas are put on the table and considered, giving confidence to team members that no stone has been left unturned. This is critical to hold each other in...

4: Accountability Teams that commit to decisions and standards of performance do not hesitate to hold one another accountable for adhering to those decisions and standards. What is more, they don't rely on the team leader as the primary source of accountability; they go directly to their peers. This matters because by doing this the team achieves...

5: Results Teams that trust one another, engage in conflict, commit to decisions, and hold one another accountable are very likely to set aside their individual needs and agendas and focus almost exclusively on what is best for the team. They do not give in to the temptation to place their departments, career aspirations, or ego-driven status ahead of the collective results that define team success.

Be a great team

Therefore a healthy team is built on a commitment to deliver results and each person on the team is ready to be part of a network of accountability for those results. Knowing that they are accountable, they commit to the decisions made by the team. That commitment is the bi-product of healthy, vigorous debate and conflict. Constructive conflict comes as a result of an environment of trust, openness and confidence.

Story 2: Simon, a law graduate with no job to go to

I studied English, economics and history at A Level and I always thought I would be a solicitor some day. For most of his working life my Dad had been in job in which he felt he had not used his brain enough. He encouraged me to pursue a profession where I would use my brain. I went to York University and although I enjoyed the course at first, I realised how competitive it was to get any internships. Roughly 900 people were applying for 50 places. I also worked for a firm of solicitors during one holiday, which I found very boring and tedious.

Towards the end of my degree course, I began to panic about what I was going to do. If it was less competitive to get into a law firm, I guess I would have just gone down that route as that was the most logical and was what

I was trained for. I had been talking about being a solicitor since I was 16. However, it was hugely competitive, so I 'panic-applied' to a random selection of graduate schemes, most of which did not interest me that much. I was unsuccessful. University had ended; I had spent three years studying something I was not going to use for the foreseeable future. I moved back home and started full time at Sainsbury's, where I had worked in the holidays, to earn some money.

This time at Sainsbury's gave me space to reflect on what I really wanted to do. After about three months, my friend David came to me with an idea for a digital music app. This was creative, innovative and I had a passion for music. It seemed very marketable and fun at the same time. A far cry from the work of a solicitor.

I moved back up to York to work on this project with David whilst covering the bills by working part time at Sainsbury's. We now have investors and a support team of accountants and legal advisors to help us build our business. This is something I have a passion for and believe in. My days at Sainsbury's are numbered, although it has been a great source of income whilst I get my business up and running.

Lessons from Simon's story

Here are some reflections from Simon's story to apply to your own career journey:

- Be open to the idea that a degree course may not be linked to the career which you finally pursue. At least you still get a degree.

- Internships/placements are incredibly valuable to give you a taster as to whether this career is for you.

- Try not to panic and apply for anything that moves. Simon's advice to anyone in that position was to give yourself time to reflect on what you really want not what you 'ought' to do.

- 'If you are really passionate about something, don't give up,' Simon told me. Find out what really interests you and go for it, even if it is not the normal route. You will get there in the end.

- Working in a supermarket for a while may be just what you need to just earn some money until the new route emerges.

Retiring and finding your niche

At the end of a long career, I can only imagine (as I am not there yet) that it must feel quite daunting for some when you first stop work. What is your identity now that you are not working? Where is your worth? What do you do with your time that has meaning and purpose? Everyone is different as to how they manage this season in their lives. Some are happy to put their feet up and focus on the grandchildren, which is a great investment. I know my life was incredibly enriched by having two sets of loving grandparents. Others, though, want to use their skills and talents a little more, maybe in a voluntary position.

This was the case for Fred who retired from a very successful job in engineering. He now works voluntarily as the wedding coordinator at his local church, where there are some 65 weddings each year. He did not find retiring an issue at all.

Story 3: Fred, on retiring

Soon after birth I had meningitis and my mother was told I was unlikely to make it through the night. I did. I was lucky to be alive. The hearing in one ear though was completely damaged. I have learned to live with this impairment and most people do not know I contend with hearing loss. Naturally it affects how I communicate with others and has an impact on which environments or positions I choose to put myself in which improve my chances of hearing.

After I completed my degree in engineering, I worked for a machine tools and robotics company. I chose to start work on the factory floor alongside other less qualified staff. No one could understand it. Why did I not go into the management training scheme straight away and earn far more money? I had learned early on that I would only put myself in positions that suited me and my limitations, where I could succeed. I soon gained my confidence and it was not long before I was promoted up the management ladder.

I became project manager and production manager for the factory, overseeing 300 staff during the height of the union disputes in the 1970s. I had teams of engineers working for me and I became well known for my organisational skills and the ability to implement a plan or project extremely well. For example, we had to introduce a new computer system, which would automatically tell you what to buy and make. I implemented this so well in our factory that, unfortunately, it backfired. The system was in place on time and correctly implemented unlike any of the other factories, yet it proved to be the reason I had to close the factory. I had done my job too well. It was heartbreaking after so many years. I had the very painful job of making people redundant.

The skills I loved using in my working career were organisational ones where I could manage a project from start to finish. Whilst I had much experience with managing teams, this aspect was not something I cherished. Being responsible for organising others who report to me I found particularly challenging with a hearing impairment, although of course I could do it. I love working in teams although I prefer to work in a 'virtual' team with a defined task to implement.

When I retired, there was plenty to keep me occupied: I enjoy photography and, of course, there are the grandchildren. I was also volunteering to help run the business affairs of the local church. It became apparent that there was a need to coordinate the roughly 65 weddings that the church conducts each year: from the moment a couple contacts the church, to organising the banns of marriage to be read, to the whole legal and practical procedure of running weddings.

The wedding-coordinator role is a classic project-management role working in a virtual team. I work 30-40 hours a week doing this job and it saves the clergy a significant amount of time and hassle, allowing them to spend more time focusing on pastoral work. The skills I learned in my career have set me up well to do this role. I learned how to write technical specifications with precision. I draw on these skills when helping couples through the process of getting married.

I am extremely privileged to be involved with couples just as they start to plan their wedding. I am very enthusiastic about my role and excited that my skills are being used to the full in my retirement.

Lessons from Fred's story

Here are some reflections from Fred's story to apply to your own career journey:

- Whatever your limitations, know what physical work environment works best for you, even if it does not make rational sense to those around you.

- Discern what relational environment works best for you. Are you more comfortable heading up a team, being part of a team or working in a virtual team? It makes a huge difference.

- Your sense of purpose may change and evolve through retirement, no doubt. I was always inspired by Eileen (83), who attended a leadership-development course I was running for a local church. Later, she was appointed to the management committee of the church, taking her Mac to meetings to take notes. She said: 'You are never too old to learn.' I want to follow her example.

- When you find the skills you love and 'cannot stop yourself from using them', you never really retire, as work becomes your hobby. A part of you comes alive when you use these skills. So while you are able, why stop using them?

JOURNEYING ON

Finding our dream job isn't necessarily easy, and for that reason it is often easier to stay where we are. Why bother to make all that effort to work out what your SHIFT pattern is? Why take the risk of trying new things when you can't be sure they will go well? Why not stick with what you know, take the simple route? Many people do just this. But there is nearly always a cost.

Feeling, at best, unfulfilled in our work, at worst, deeply distressed, erodes our confidence and destroys our sense of wellbeing. And few of us can hermetically seal the impact of these feelings and thoughts into our work life: they spill over into every area of life and begin to impact others. There is a cost involved in shifting gear and finding your dream job, but there is nearly always a cost to not doing this as well.

I hope this book has given you some tools to work with, practical ways to explore what your dream role might be. I hope it has also given you some inspiration to start through the stories of other people who have taken that journey and found roles that better suit who they are and what they have to offer.

There are no guarantees. The journey can be tough. And ultimately none of us knows how long we've got. Yet the journey is an adventure, with excitement and challenges on the way. For most people it begins with a simple decision, a decision to take the first step. Why not make that decision today?

Endnotes

[i] James Lawrence, *Growing Leaders* (BRF, 2014), p.25

[ii] Ibid, p.24

[iii] It is worth noting that research is emerging to suggest that, due to the significant gap in circumstances between younger and older generations today, more and more people are seeking mentors in their peer groups rather than generations above them. This is because they feel there is more understanding of the financial pressures, socio-economic pressures and so on that might never have been experienced by those 10-20 years older. So don't assume you will find your best mentor in somebody many years older. You may find somebody very close in age to you. It has more to do with the number of years' experience they have in the career or business you are passionate about.

[iv] Richard Bolles, *What Colour is My Parachute?* (Ten Speed , 2016)

[v] Adapted from Daniel Porot's diagram in Richard Bolles, *What Colour is My Parachute?* (Ten Speed Press, 2016), p.142 and used with the permission of Daniel Porot.

[vi] If you are considering a coaching career I would highly recommend you investigate a course at either The Gestalt Centre, London *(www.gestaltcentre.org)* or Metanoia, London (www.metanoia.org). There is also a range of coaching master programmes run by organisations such as Henley and Ashridge Management Schools.

[vii] Adapted from John Lees, *How to Get a Job You Love* (McGraw-Hill Professional, 2012), p.82

[viii] Adapted from Richard Bolles, *What Colour is My Parachute?* (Ten Speed Press, 2016), p.61. A copy of this checklist is available in a digital format from the website *www.shift-direction.com.*

[ix] Adapted from John Lees, *How to Get a Job You Love* (McGraw-Hill Professional, 2012), p.40. A copy of this checklist is available in a digital format from the website *www.shift-direction.com.*

[x] Adapted from John Lees, *How to Get a Job You Love* (McGraw-Hill Professional, 2012), p.14. A copy of this checklist is available in a digital format from the website *www.shift-direction.com.*

[xi] Richard Bolles, *What Colour is My Parachute?* (Ten Speed Press, 2016), p.225

[xii] John Lees, *How to Get a Job You Love* (McGraw-Hill Professional, 2012), p.27

[xiii] Richard Bolles, *What Colour is My Parachute?* (Ten Speed Press, 2016), p.184

[xiv] William Bridges, *Managing Transitions* (Nicholas Brealey, 2009)

[xv] James Lawrence and Simon Heathfield, *Growing Leaders* (CPAS, 2008)

[xvi] Patrick Lencioni, *The Five Dysfunctions of a Team* (John Wiley and Sons, 2002)

10508298R00082

Printed in Germany
by Amazon Distribution
GmbH, Leipzig